Modern Japan

2-6.75

Titles in this series

MODERN TIMES

Modern Japan

Barry Williams

SHERBORNE SCHOOL FOR GIRLS, DORSET

LONGMAN

LONGMAN GROUP LIMITED
LONDON
Associated companies, branches and representatives throughout the world

© Longman Group Ltd 1969

First published 1969
Fourth impression 1974
ISBN 0 582 20437 2

Printed in Great Britain by
Lowe & Brydone (Printers) Ltd, Thetford, Norfolk

To Ann, Sara and Jane

Preface

What do you associate with the name 'Japan'? In the 1960s words like transistors and colour television, cameras and giant oil tankers, the Toyota motor-car and the Honda motor-cycle might come to mind. Yet before and during the Second World War older readers will recall a brutal image—of the hated Japanese soldier and the suicide pilots. This was the period of the 'Yellow Menace', of Japanese imperialism and cheap industrial goods.

Sixty years ago there had been a different idea of Japan. She was a respected nation, an ally of Britain and possessor of a well-disciplined and trained army and navy. (Compare the cartoons on pages 36 and 106.) However, just over a century ago the reader, had he been alive, would have pictured a feudal country where foreigners, the 'hairy barbarians', were treated with hostility.

This book is an attempt to describe and explain the rapid process by which Japan modernized herself. The subject is a vast one and I have only highlighted some of the significant events and developments. But the reader will find many aspects of modern Japan given some attention: the economic and social as well as the political and military.

This is not in any way an original work on the subject, and I must acknowledge a great debt to authorities on Japan like Richard Storry, W. G. Beasley, F. C. Jones, Sir George Sansom, R. P. Dore, John Embree, G. C. Allen and W. W. Lockwood.

My aim has been to provide a younger generation of readers with an interesting, accurate and up-to-date account of Japan during the last hundred years or so. With an age group of fifteen to eighteen in mind, I hope the book will be found suitable for both specific study and general reading.

Acknowledgements

The author wishes to thank Professor Geoffrey Bownas of the Centre of Japanese Studies, Sheffield University, both for his encouragement and for his constructive comments on the manuscript.

Also the author acknowledges his debt to the Director of the Peace Museum, Hiroshima, for his help; to Routledge and Kegan Paul for permission to use extensively the sociological researches of R. P. Dore (*City Life in Japan*, 1951) and John Embree (*A Japanese Village*, 1946); and to Mr. A. R. C. Brown for his cartographical advice.

We are grateful to the following for permission to reproduce copyright material: Jonathan Cape Ltd for an extract from *Warrior Without Weapons* translated by Edward Fitzgerald; J. M. Dent & Sons, Ltd., and W. W. Norton & Co. Inc., for extracts from *Climax At Midway* by T. V. Tuleja, © 1960 by Thaddeus V. Tuleja; Hutchinson Publishing Group Ltd and United States Naval Institute for an extract from *Midway* by Fuchida and Okumiya, Copyright © 1955 by U.S. Naval Institute, Annapolis; Routledge & Kegan Paul, Ltd., for extracts from *A Japanese Village* by J. F. Embree and extracts from *City Life in Japan* by R. P. Dore.

For permission to reproduce photographs we are grateful to the following: Associated Press Ltd.: pages 75, 86 and 109; Black Star Publishing Co. Ltd.: pages 115 and 126; Cresset Press, *The Phoenix Cup* by John Morris 1947: page 122; Illustrated London News: pages 10, 14, 17, 20, 22, 25, 30, 39, 40, 51, 59, 67, 69 and 84; Imperial War Museum: pages 103, 114 and 119; Japan Information Centre: pages 8, 131, 137, 140 and 142; Keystone Press Agency Ltd: pages 108 and 124; J. B. Lippincott Company, *The March of Japan* by Edgar Lajtha 1936: page 77; London Express News and Feature Services: page 127; Roy Mellars: page 118; Samuel E. Morison, *United States Naval Operations* Volume 4: page 98; Official U.S. Navy Photograph: pages 92, 97 and 101; The Overseas Construction Association of Japan: pages 139 and 143; Paul Popper Ltd.: page 116; Punch: pages 33, 34, 36, 70, 83 and 106; Radio Times Hulton Picture Library: page 29; Routledge and Kegan Paul Ltd., *City Life in Japan* by R. P. Dore 1958: pages 133 and 134 and *A Japanese Village* by John Embree 1946: pages 57, 61 and 64; Asahi Shimbunsha *This Is Japan* by Kinsuke Shinada: page 141; Weidenfeld and Nicholson, *The Modern History of Japan* by W. G. Beasley: page 86.

The cover photograph is reproduced by kind permission of Ishikawajima-Harima Heavy Industries Co. Ltd.

For permission to base maps and diagrams on theirs we are grateful to the following:
Page 6: Weidenfeld and Nicolson, from *The Modern History of Japan* by W. G. Beasley 1963; page 42: Jarrolds, from *Admiral Togo* by G. Blond 1961; page 50: Illustrated London News; pages 56 and 62: Routledge and Kegan Paul from *A Japanese Village* by John Embree 1940; page 91: Little and Brown, from *History of U.S. Naval Operations* Volume 3 by Samuel E. Morison; page 100: H.M.S.O. Official War History, from *War at Sea 1939–1945* Volume 2 by S. W. Roskill; page 130: R. P. Dore *City Life in Japan* published by Routledge and Kegan Paul 1958.

Contents

Contents

Contents

1 The Black Ships of 1853

Although it was midsummer the seas to the east of Honshu, the main island of Japan, were covered in a thin mist. The Japanese authorities in Yedo (the old name for Tokyo) watched anxiously for the first sign of American ships. Dutch merchants had warned the Japanese that some were coming, but exactly when and how many were guesswork. Rumours spread that 'one hundred thousand devils with white faces' were coming to crush Japan. Then, on 8 July 1853, the 'black ships of the evil men' appeared out of the mists, travelling at eight knots into Uraga Bay, just at the head of the great stretch of water leading to Yedo.

There were only four ships and a mere 560 men, but they created a sensation. Two of them, the *Mississippi* and the *Susquehanna* were very modern, steam-powered frigates—most Japanese had never seen or heard of such ships. From the deck of one of them Francis Hawks saw some broad-sailed fishing junks: the fishermen were shouting and pulling in their nets with great haste, then they rowed frantically to the shore 'like wild birds at a sudden intruder', wrote Hawks.

In command of this American expedition was Commodore Matthew Perry—'Old Matt' to his crews. He was a vain, overbearing man, and he refused to deal with the minor officials sent by the Japanese government to meet him, and who tried in vain to persuade him to go away. He told them he would only see the Governor of the area. This was finally arranged and a short man in gold-coloured trousers and varnished clogs looking, Hawks said, 'like an unusually brilliant jack of trumps' came on board for a glass of champagne. But when Perry finally went ashore on 14 July neither side was taking any chances. The American squadron had its decks cleared for action, whilst 5,000 Japanese troops, 'encased in ribbed armour of leather and iron', stood on guard. In a specially erected building Perry, with great solemnity, handed over to the Japanese a letter from the American President addressed to the Mikado, the Emperor of Japan. In friendly terms it requested protection for shipwrecked seamen, coaling ports for American traders in the Pacific and some trading rights. Perry, however, added a covering letter of his own which amounted to an ultimatum: he would return 'with a much larger force' in the following

Commodore Matthew Perry: a Japanese painting 1854

spring for a reply. Then, defying Japanese wishes, he steamed up the shore line to Yedo before turning out into the north Pacific.

But Perry did not know that the Emperor himself had no power to grant what the Americans wanted. For many hundreds of years the real ruler of Japan had been the Shogun, the emperor's senior military commander, who controlled affairs from his headquarters in Yedo Castle and was helped by a group of administrative officials called the Bakufu. The emperor lived inland at Kyoto. He had become cut off from day-to-day government and was more like a political figurehead.

So it was the Shogun who received Perry's letters. He read them and called a council meeting. He was asked, 'Is the Mikado's court at Kyoto informed of these barbarians' arrival?' The Shogun said yes, and in reply to a further query on the court's attitude answered: 'The Emperor has ordered prayers at all sanctuaries for a typhoon from Heaven to save our country as in the days of the danger from the Mongols.' Clearly not much practical help in dealing with the Americans could be expected from the Emperor. But the chances of the Bakufu taking a strong line were equally doubtful, because at a further meeting council members were informed, 'If you saw the treasury accounts you would be startled, and would learn at a glance the hopelessness of going to war.'

Perry returned in February 1854 with his promised larger force—9 ships and 250 mounted guns—and he had no difficulty in completing negotiations for a treaty. Signed on 31 March 1854 it opened two small ports to American ships and said shipwrecked sailors would receive protection. The Japanese thought they were just playing for time. 'We are without a navy and our coasts are undefended. Our policy shall be to evade any definite answer', said the Bakufu. But subsequent events were to prove, says one historian, that 'it was only the beginning of a many-sided invasion by the West which was to have consequences beyond the wildest fears or dreams of any who lived in Yedo on that day.'

Fears? dreams? Why the original hostility and talk of war?

3

What was Perry doing there anyway? The next two chapters will look at a country which had deliberately kept out foreigners for over two hundred years; and at the reasons for the confusion and the agony of many Japanese when faced with the American demands in 1853.

2 The Closed Country

Japan goes into isolation

In 1640 the Japanese government issued the following edict: 'Any Christian bold enough to come to Japan, even if he be the god of the Christians himself, shall pay for it with his head.' In the same year some Portuguese arrived from Macao, a trading settlement in China. All but thirteen were executed and those spared were sent back to their employers with the words, 'Let them think no more of us.'

The Japanese themselves were already forbidden to leave the country under pain of death should they return. Japan had suddenly and drastically cut herself off from the rest of the world. For the next two hundred years only the Dutch managed to persuade the Japanese to grant them a tiny trading concession, and even this was on an island in Nagasaki harbour far away from Yedo. Here they were fenced in with iron spikes and had guards on the bridge which led to the mainland.

In this 'closed country' a semi-feudal government sought to preserve its power for ever. Strictly 'feudal' is a word historians use to describe the granting of a fief or area of land by a lord to his vassal in return for military service; but it has also come to mean, more loosely, a society where peasants cultivate the land and pay taxes in goods or in services to the local lord and not to a central government. Japanese feudalism had developed over many centuries and reached its highest point at roughly the same time as in western Europe, namely A.D. 1100. But by the seventeenth and eighteenth centuries circumstances were changing, however hard the authorities in Yedo tried to freeze society.

In theory Japanese society was divided into four distinct classes. In order of social importance they were soldiers, farmers, artisans or town workers and traders. No man was supposed to rise above the class into which he was born.

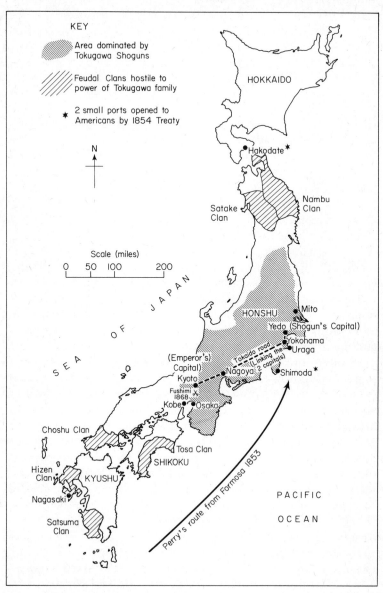

Feudal Japan (about 1850)

There were also many social outcasts called *eta* who had no accepted place in Japanese life and who spent a miserable existence usually as beggars. The samurai or warrior class formed a powerful ruling aristocracy, and it was their duty to protect and administer the country. The vast mass of Japanese were peasants, and as farmers their duty in society was rice cultivation. The third class was small and comprised the few artisans who worked on useful handicrafts in the towns. But the merchant, who tried to make a profit from trade, was despised by the other three classes because he produced nothing.

However, in no country can the social class divisions remain completely rigid. There may be stresses not only between classes but also within them. So let us look at each class more closely.

The Samurai

There were nearly half a million samurai families who, with their 270 overlords or *daimyo*, were scattered in their fiefs throughout Japan. Nominally these feudal lords owed their loyalty to the Mikado in Kyoto, but since 1603 they were dominated by the great Tokugawa family. The head of this family was by custom appointed Shogun, who, as we have seen, exercised on behalf of the Mikado absolute authority in Japan. An able Shogun meant an efficient central government. Unfortunately some of the Tokugawas were feeble rulers, easily swayed by other people, so that important positions in the Bakufu were often given to men who had little administrative ability but much personal influence.

Local *daimyo* remote from Yedo soon found that this kind of government was ineffective and slow, and they seized the chance of increasing their power in their own area. It was to stop these men seeking even greater power by appealing for foreign help that the 1640 edict was passed.

The samurai were far from being a united class. There were those who were closely connected with the *daimyo's* own family, by blood or long service, and they used this to make themselves rich and to own land of their own. Below them were the middle-rank samurai who found that in practice they were

7

excluded from the most important positions of power. For every fief had a castle-fortress (see the picture below), with many posts to be filled; these ranged from advisers to the *daimyo* and governing a local district to service as guards or messengers. Then there were the thousands of lesser samurai who just performed military duty as foot-soldiers.

A gulf developed between these different samurai in their standard of living, especially as the more important had high incomes. Instead of money a *koku* of rice was used as the standard medium of exchange, i.e. like we use a £ note; a *koku* measured five bushels and was reckoned to feed one person for one year. Different samurai incomes ranged from 10,000 *koku* to 20 *koku*.

The widespread discontent amongst samurai was made worse by the *ronin*. They were samurai who had no *daimyo*. In the seventeenth century some dangerous samurai had had their land taken away; these men and their retainers became adventurers or ruffians much feared for their constant brawling.

To keep control in these conditions was a difficult task for the Bakufu in Yedo. The power to take away a *daimyo's* land was one important weapon in the hands of the Shogun. The Tokugawas controlled 40 per cent of the usable land in Japan, and as it was concentrated in central Honshu it meant that

A *daimyo's* castle of Tokugawa times. The walls are rather obscure behind the trees

Yedo and Kyoto, the two 'capitals', were firmly in the family grasp. Another way the Tokugawas kept control was through 'alternate attendance'. Richard Storry, the historian, has called this a 'permanent hostage system', because every *daimyo* was by law forced to live for six months alternately in his fief and in the Shogun's headquarters. When his six months in Yedo were up he had to leave his wife and family there whilst he went back to his fief. This way the Shogun had hostages for the *daimyo's* good behaviour. Yet rebellion was an ever-present nightmare for the Shogun, and it was a standing order that the Yedo guards 'watch for guns going in and women going out', for a *daimyo* would certainly try to get his family away before supporting a revolt.

The Peasants

Around 1800 the population of Japan was thirty million; of these the overwhelming majority were unfree, poverty-stricken peasants. They lived in villages which were self-sufficient, and their chief source of wealth was the cultivation of rice. But as 40 per cent to 60 per cent of a peasant household's rice production was annually taken by the *daimyo* in taxes to support himself and his large number of retainers, the peasants' standard of living was low. Many had harsh lords. One visited his estates in 1640 after a ten-year absence, and finding the villagers in well-built houses instead of hovels said, 'These people are too comfortable. They must be more heavily taxed.' This attitude of mind was not exceptional as can be seen from an order to villages that went out in 1649: 'Husbands must work in the fields and wives must work at the loom. However good-looking a wife may be, if she neglects her household duties by drinking or sightseeing or rambling over the hillsides, she must be divorced.' Some lords were humane and others had lazy officials, but there was little chance of a peasant raising his standard of living.

A village had about fifty households, and the usual area of ground a family had to cultivate was two-and-a-half acres or ten *tan* in Japanese measurement. Enormous labour was involved. At least five men would have to work hard for a year on a family's ten *tan* to produce ten *koku* of rice—and even that depended on good soil and adequate rainfall for the paddy fields. The feudal tax to the *daimyo* took half; and occasional, arbitrary taxes on doors, windows, female children or hazel trees would take a further proportion. The plight of a peasant at times became so bad that he gave some of his ten *tan* to a money-lender as security for an immediate loan. Legally this was forbidden, so the peasant found himself still liable for the feudal tax on land he had already given away!

Records of the eighteenth and early nineteenth centuries show periods of appalling disasters. In one decade: 200,000 deaths in the 1773 plague; floods and a volcanic eruption in 1778; a five-year famine because of crop failure; annual typhoons. A contemporary description by a samurai in one

Japanese costumes sketched in Nagasaki in 1854

province said: 'The loss of life through starvation in this northern province was dreadful. There was nothing to eat but horseflesh, and when this ran short dogs and cats. In some villages of thirty to fifty households not one person survived. Corpses were unburied and had to be eaten by beasts and birds.'

Thus taxation, harsh landlords, primitive methods of agriculture and natural disasters meant a bitter life of poverty for the Japanese peasant. What was wretched in good rice-production years became unbearable in lean years. In the eighteenth century we have records of over a thousand riots among the peasants; and in the same century the custom of *mabiki* grew up—this means the process of 'thinning out' by families which could not afford to feed all their children. Such infanticide, by leaving unwanted babies exposed on a nearby hillside, gives you an idea of the despair of the Japanese peasantry.

This picture of both samurai and peasant life was generally true over the period 1600 to 1850. On the surface there was little change, and the feudal overlords of Japan were content that their power should remain complete for ever. But in the towns the pattern of life was changing.

The Artisans and Merchants

Kyoto had once been the largest city in Japan, but by 1850 Yedo had grown in three centuries from a small fishing village to a city of three-quarters of a million. Retainers of the *daimyo*, compelled to spend half a year there, swelled this figure by another twenty-five thousand. Osaka with its quarter-million people was the centre of Japanese commerce. In these towns numerous skilled crafts were carried on, such as furniture- and sword-making, and the weaving of fine silk and cotton in a wide variety of design and colour. These handicrafts were encouraged by enterprising merchants who were not slow to find new markets amongst the more wealthy samurai. This stimulated what economists call an 'expanding economy'. If the demand for more and different kinds of goods could be met, the resulting increase in the number of jobs available would raise the ordinary townspeople's standard of living.

Many merchants, although playing a vital part in this expanding economy by bringing together the 'producers' and 'consumers' of goods, gained a bad reputation for making enormous profits for themselves. One merchant, arrested in Yedo in the 1830s on charges of disloyalty and corruption, was found to be an ex-peasant who had taken a job in the Yedo Mint where the little coinage used in cash sales in the towns was made. A search of his house revealed immense hoards of gold and silver coins, and that he employed twenty maids and thirty-two manservants! Men of this sort clearly had no part in the kind of society the Tokugawa Shoguns wanted.

The Osaka traders were not just merchants; they became money-lenders as well. Throughout the eighteenth century the use of coins became more common. In a country organized with rice as the standard of wealth this was yet another idea which did not fit in with the Shogun's view of feudal Japan. Samurai, we have seen, received their 'pay' in bundles of rice measured in so many *koku*. They found it convenient to sell any surplus in the great Osaka rice market for cash (cash was much more useful than awkward packets of rice during their six months in Yedo). By the nineteenth century many samurai had got into the habit of borrowing money in Osaka, using *future* rice income as security. The aristocracy in debt to the despised merchant! Some strange things were happening which thoughtful Japanese did not like.

Bakufu Incompetence

So when the American, Perry, arrived in 1853 there were already many developments inside Japan which the Bakufu neither understood nor knew how to control. First, there were the restless *daimyo* and their feudal clans in the outlying provinces; secondly, many of the samurai were in deep debt; thirdly, peasant risings were becoming very common, and the *ronin* were leading riots when a rice harvest was poor. And now some Japanese scholars, searching through old manuscripts, found accounts of an earlier and glorious Japan under the direct rule of the emperors. Whisperers, who said that the Shogun and the Bakufu were incompetent, suggested that the Emperor should be restored to his ancestral powers to lead the Japanese people in a revival of their past greatness.

For the Shogun 1853 was the crisis point. How would he deal with the 'foreign devils'?

3 What About the Foreign Devils?

Foreign Interest in Japan

By the mid-nineteenth century many westerners (i.e. Europeans and Americans) were anxious that Japan's closed door be opened or broken down. The Dutch had won their small foothold, but the Russians, Britons and Americans were still for different reasons trying to get trading concessions. A British journal, *The Edinburgh Review* took a high moral tone when in October 1852 it wrote: 'The compulsory seclusion of the Japanese is wrong, not only to themselves, but to the civilized world.' And British traders agreed. In 1840, in the Opium War with China, Britain forced open some Chinese ports as far north as Shanghai. This point was only 500 miles from Nagasaki, so Japan seemed on the fringe of the traders' next area of expansion. As early as 1808 a British warship had bombarded its way into Nagasaki harbour and demanded stores at gunpoint. Merchants were thus well aware of what methods to use.

The Russian government was showing interest in Japan for trade, for it was slowly extending its territorial power in the Amur River region, on the mainland just across the Sea of Japan.

The Americans also were concerned in the north Pacific in the early nineteenth century. In 1837 a private ship, the *Morrison*, with Bibles and trade goods, entered Yedo Bay and had hordes of Japanese sightseers on board immediately it anchored. The next day, however, shore-guns opened fire and the sailing ship made a hasty retreat. Then in the 1850s the American government took up the issue. The Pacific coast of

How the Japanese saw the British in the mid-nineteenth century. 'John Bull' and his wife, the 'western barbarians'

the United States was developing rapidly, especially when California was gained from Mexico in 1848. Japan suddenly became an important stage on the direct route from San Francisco to Shanghai which the new Pacific Mail S.S. Company was using.

In Chapter 1 we noted the supply and hospitality terms of Perry's letter to the Emperor; the reasons for this can now be seen. Japanese coastal waters would be part of major American shipping lanes to the Far East, and a refuelling point was necessary in the early steamship era. There was another factor. Seventeen million American dollars had already been invested in north Pacific whaling, and crews of these ships wrecked in typhoons would need shelter—not the execution promised in the 1640 edict!

The Decline of the Bakufu

The Bakufu did not like this interest. They took it for granted that the foreigners were bent on conquest, though not all the *daimyo* agreed. The Shogun and the Bakufu should have taken a clear course of action, yet one Japanese wrote, 'From the day of Perry's arrival for more than ten years, our country was in a state of indescribable confusion. The government was weak and irresolute, without power of decision.' In 1853, immediately Perry arrived, the Bakufu showed its weakness by asking the advice of the main feudal lords near Yedo. In general the replies took the line that as 'shogun' meant 'queller of barbarians' he should get on with his job. But as we have seen the Shogun gave in, and the treaty opening two small ports to the Americans was signed. An American consul, Townshend Harris, then arrived, and after much obstruction from the Japanese authorities managed to get the Bakufu to extend these trading privileges to other ports. The scramble was on, within five years the Bakufu had been bullied into signing treaties with the United States, Russia, Britain and France. The terms were very one-sided:
1. Yedo and other ports were open to foreign traders.
2. Only low import charges could be made on foreign goods.
3. Foreign citizens were exempt from Japanese law.

The outcry from the *daimyo* was loud and clear. The Bakufu was attacked as 'the betrayer of the national interest' to 'hairy foreigners', and in the next forty years the Japanese were to devote much energy in getting these 'unequal treaties' revised. But first the Shogun and the Bakufu had to be got rid of. The senior member of the Shogun's council, Ii, who had signed the treaties was assassinated. Other members of the Bakufu had their lives threatened by indignant *daimyo*, and the blackmail worked. In October 1862 the rule of a lord's alternate attendance at court and in his fief was virtually ended. Without this rule the Tokugawas could exercise little control. As one contemporary Japanese put it: 'And so in the space of one morning the prestige of the Tokugawa family, that had day and night 80,000 vassals at its beck and call, fell to ruin.'

Clash of Opinion

It was easy to shout down the Bakufu; it was not so easy to find an acceptable alternative policy. From well before Perry's arrival until the mid 1860s three main points of view, each with many supporters, expressed different answers to the question, 'What are we to do about the foreign devils?' Let the Japanese speak for themselves.

'The heirs of the Great Sun have occupied the Imperial Throne from generation to generation without change from time immemorial. Today the alien barbarians of the west are dashing about across the seas trampling other countries underfoot, and daring with their squinting eyes and limping feet to override the noble nations. What manner of arrogance is this!' This was the viewpoint of the influential feudal clan of Lord Mito who lived to the north of Yedo. He adopted a slogan *Son-no Jo-i*, which meant 'Honour the Emperor and Expel the Barbarians'. It spelt doom to the Bakufu as it would lead to the restoration of the Mikado to his ruling position of centuries ago.

The Mito 'school' had many supporters in the old feudal families; but young samurai thought Lord Mito was a selfish, ambitious man, merely wishing to replace the Tokugawas with the Mito family. There were plenty of talented young samurai, and they took up a second rallying cry: 'Eastern ethics and western science', made popular by a samurai named Sakuma. He wrote about Perry's men:

'Their manner of expression was exceedingly arrogant and the resulting insult to our national dignity was not small. Those who heard could but gnash their teeth.'

Sakuma wanted the widespread education of the Japanese people on traditional eastern lines. They would be instructed in things like Confucius's rules of conduct which stressed the obedience of a son to his father and the care a ruler should

Samurai in traditional costume in 1864. Notice the curious sword sheaths

have for his people. At the same time Japanese scholars must make a rapid study of western scientific ideas, so that Japan could meet the foreigners' challenge on equal terms. Sakuma himself set an example by learning how to cast cannon and use them. He also pressed for the translation of Dutch books into Japanese using an old Chinese proverb as justification: 'to know one's enemy and know oneself brings constant victory.' But such western ideas were dangerous. Sakuma was assassinated by a fanatical Mito supporter in 1864.

A small but important third group favoured opening the country completely and basing Japan's future on western civilization. Even before 1853 a few men managed to evade the seclusion laws and go abroad to America and Europe. 'I learned something of the postal system and military conscription and a perplexing institution called representative government', wrote one of them. However, fear of assassination kept these few men out of the struggle for power until after 1868.

1868

This was the critical year. In all this confusion it only needed a small number of strong-willed men to seize the initiative. In 1868 a group of *daimyo* of the Choshu and Satsuma clans from the far south-west of Japan made their bid for power. For some years they had been reforming their own armies and navies on European lines. Drill, arms and uniform showed the influence of British and French ideas. Also they took on volunteers from the towns and peasantry, which meant an end to the rigid Japanese military tradition whereby only the samurai could bear arms. What they were doing looked very much like rebellion, so they found the Mito slogan, *Son-no Jo-i* very useful. When they also adopted the ancient chrysanthemum banner of the Imperial House support grew. The Choshu and Satsuma were joined in an anti-Bakufu alliance first by some rich Osaka merchants like the Mitsui family, and then by a few members of the Emperor's Kyoto court.

The show-down came in January 1868. In a three-day battle at Fushimi on the road from Osaka to Kyoto the Bakufu forces made a last, desperate attempt to keep their power. But the discipline of the Choshu and Satsuma armies proved too much. The soldiers of the Shogun retreated in disorder.

The Japanese call 1868 'The Year of the Restoration'— that is the restoration of the Emperor to his proper powers in the state.

4 Japan Modernizes

New Men and New Ideas

The men who seized power in 1868 had found the slogan 'Expel the Barbarians' a valuable way of getting support; but once in the government they paid little heed to the idea. The Emperor Meiji set the tone in his proclamation to the Japanese people only two months after the battle of Fushimi, 'Knowledge must be sought from all over the world.' In the same year he marked the return of emperors to public life by moving his court from Kyoto to Yedo and renaming the city, Tokyo, meaning Eastern Capital.

In the next thirty years Japan was modernized from a relatively backward semi-feudal state into one capable of winning a modern war against a European country. How was it done?

The foundations were laid by men who for years had pressed for the study of western achievements. They found that whereas before 1868 they were likely to be assassinated for their views, after 1868 they had government support. Japan was now led by men of honesty and ability from the samurai aristocracy, and more particularly from the heads of the Choshu and Satsuma clans. These were the men who provided the drive to revolutionize Japanese life. They had a remarkable gift for seeking out ideas from the West and adapting them to Japanese life. Some of their schemes meant large-scale reorganization and they showed an equal capacity here for boldness and efficiency. Two early actions illustrate this.

First, in 1871 feudal control of land was abolished. All land came under the Emperor's authority, which meant that the *daimyo* gave up their right to have their own law courts and private armies. They stayed on, however, in their areas as Governors of Provinces, and were paid a salary by the Imperial government. The remaining samurai were also given an income, but it was very small. So large numbers of them joined the new national army, became government officials or went into business in the towns.

Second, in 1873 a new land-tax system was introduced. All land was to be 'valued': this meant fixing the amount of money that a certain area of land would fetch if sold. Then the owner paid an annual tax of 3 per cent in cash on this value. It was something quite new to Japan and there was much grumbling. Tax collectors made no allowance for a bad harvest, so the money had to be borrowed or the land would be confiscated. Records show that money-lenders charged a high rate of interest—13 per cent over only five years—and that a quarter of a million small landowners failed to pay the land-tax in the 1880s and so lost their property.

However, the benefits to Japan as a whole were soon made clear. A central, modernized taxation system gave the government stability, and with a regular source of income it could introduce some expensive yet beneficial schemes. New banks, telegraph and post offices, the new Osaka Mint, a new coinage based on the 'yen', coastal trading facilities like harbours, lighthouses and dockyards all made their appearance in the next two decades.

The Ginza, Tokyo's main shopping centre, in 1904

Then in 1881 the Japanese government found a financial administrator of genius, Count Matsukata. He made a determined effort to introduce order into a difficult financial situation, and by careful national housekeeping he reduced the government's annual debt from 245 million yen to a startling 5 million yen within ten years.

Japan's Industrial Revolution

The pioneers of Japan's industrial revolution received much support from the government. One family business, for instance, formed a company called the Mitsubishi, and with loans from the government opened a large trade with China; then with the profits it bought and developed the Nagasaki shipyards and invested in several gold and silver mines. In thirty years the Mitsubishi grew into a huge financial empire, and some other families like the Mitsui from Osaka followed their example. Together they formed an important feature of modern Japan—the *zaibatsu* or money cliques.

But producing all sorts of industrial goods was useless unless a market for them could be found. Enterprising Japanese business men quickly saw that the standard of living of the peasants must be raised so that they would have a little extra cash to buy the goods. Economists call this the 'growth of a rural cash income' and without it Japan could not have industrialized so quickly. Two things got the process going: fish and silk. For centuries the Japanese peasant had been completely dependent on the success of his rice crop for his living. Now, between 1870 and 1890 coastal villages turned to fishing instead of rice production as their main occupation. The *zaibatsu* loaned them money at low rates of interest so that they could buy better boats and equipment for deep-sea fishing.

In the same years a great boom in silk production took place. A peasant household had always done a little work on silk—the farmer reared silkworms in his sheds and grew mulberry trees for the worm food, whilst his wife reeled the silk on simple instruments. A few areas like Kyoto specialized in the more difficult weaving. Then in the 1860s a silkworm disease struck Europe, and suddenly a world market turned its eyes to Japan for cocoons and silk. The Japanese took their chance and industrialized. In 1870 the first 'filature' or silk-mill using machinery was opened. Government grants were given and the production of silk multiplied by five in a quarter of a century. The peasant still produced his rice, but he sent his daughters to work in a nearby mill. This meant a little spare cash in the family's pocket.

The government also encouraged modernization in farming. Students of agriculture were sent abroad and attempts were made to open up the cold and barren Hokkaido Island of

A roadside scene in rural Japan 1894

northern Japan. Irrigation schemes and the use of fertilizers were an immediate success so that rice yields per acre went up 20 per cent in as many years.

But there were problems. The population was rising and the old 2·5 acre average size of a farmer's holding dropped by 1900 to 1·2 acres. Many owners as we have seen could not meet the taxation demands, and they became tenants working the same acreage but having the added burden of rent to pay. The abolition of feudalism had done nothing for many Japanese peasants. A traveller described the older people as 'strange, gnarled creatures'. The only raincoat, he went on to say, was 'a straw cape which gave the impression of a porcupine'. Some richer landowners and the towns were benefiting from industrialization, but for the peasant-tenant life in a Japanese village changed little.

Service to the State

In 1889 the Emperor Meiji ceremoniously handed the Prime Minister a constitution. This was the first written set of rules for government that Japan had ever had, but unlike so many European constitutions which had been granted only after rebellions, this one was 'the gracious gift' of an emperor to his loyal subjects. It clearly stated that the Emperor was 'sacred and inviolable', and so he was above the problems of ordinary government. Japan was given a parliament called a Diet, but the House of Representatives was elected only by property owners—half a million out of Japan's forty million—and it had no real voice for instance in the country's budget, in which all the important money decisions would be made. Real power in Japan stayed where it had been since 1868—with the Cabinet of ex-samurai aristocracy. As far as the ordinary people were concerned, the constitution expressly said that the duties of a subject were two-fold: paying taxes and serving in the armed forces.

The idea of serving the State was given another boost by the Rescript on Education of 1890. This Imperial document gave the government very close control over Japanese education. Teachers in state schools became civil servants, teaching from textbooks officially written by the Ministry of Education. In future years we shall see how this power could be used for propaganda reasons, yet more immediately it was an important means of getting across an elementary education. Compulsory education in Japan had been established in 1872. 54,000 schools were to be built. Within half a century most people could read and write; in fact Japan became the most literate country in Asia.

The government found a new slogan to replace the old focus

A primary school of the 1880s

of local feudal loyalties. 'A Rich Country and a Strong Army' was a cry all Japanese could support. Hard work for the first and iron discipline with a willingness to die for the Emperor for the second developed over the years into a powerful brand of patriotism.

How these Changes were received

Many of these changes were so ambitious that it took many years to see their full effect. Meanwhile not all Japanese accepted modernization with enthusiasm. To some the word 'modern' equalled 'western', and they were hostile to what this might mean. Peasant opposition to some reforms was violent. The building of schools and the reform of the calendar were regarded with suspicion, but vaccination, land surveys and the numbering of houses were things which led to wide-spread rioting. It was rumoured that the last was a preliminary to the seizure by the government of all wives and daughters! Yet another rumour said the telegraph wires were being used to transmit the blood of newly-conscripted peasant soldiers, so that the Army could dye its blankets scarlet. In the 1870s alone 190 serious peasant risings were recorded.

At the other extreme it became a sort of fashion to worship everything western. 'The Civilization Ball Song' was specially

Japan's progress in 'Civilisation': the craze for western fashions shown here in a sketch done in 1875

composed for children in 1878 to impress upon their young minds the advantages of western culture. A child counted the bounces of a ball whilst reciting ten worthwhile things Japan had copied from the West:

> One for gas lamps,
> Two for steam engines,
> Three for horse-carriages,
> Four for cameras,
> Five for telegrams,
> Six for lightning-conductors,
> Seven for newspapers,
> Eight for schools,
> Nine for letter-post,
> Ten for steam-boats.

On 1 November 1882 a giant department store in Tokyo's shopping centre, the Ginza, was opened with a 2,000 candle-power arclight. Night after night thousands came to see this 'marvel of western Civilization'. In a newspaper of 1871 a new Tokyo municipal law was given the headline 'No Nakedness'. It was directed at the rickshaw men who were ordered to cover themselves with more than a loin-cloth. 'You must not', said the newspaper, 'be laughed at by foreigners.'

5   Bushido

The Way of the Warrior

Bushido is Japanese for 'the way of the warrior'. The word itself became well known inside Japan only in the 1890s, but the ideas behind it go far back into Japanese history and were gathered together in the middle of the seventeenth century into a kind of code of behaviour. This code had a strong influence on the Japanese ruling class, the samurai, and after 1868 both the Army and State officials tried to live up to the ideals of *bushido*. They did this with great success, but as we shall see in a later chapter, in the 1930s and '40s the 'way of the warrior' changed, and Japan became bitterly hated abroad.

There were four essential features of this code: chivalry, courage, honour and loyalty. The first had its beginnings in medieval times when the Japanese warrior class, like the knights of western European feudalism, was the only important source of defence and law and order in the country. The samurai were expected to behave with courtesy and politeness to civilians, and to show sympathy and pity for a defeated enemy. 'Spare all who surrender, but destroy all who refuse' was an old Japanese maxim which found its way into the code.

The second feature, courage, was what all soldiers, Japanese or not, were expected to possess, but *bushido* extended it to an indifference to death. The Japanese say this gives a soldier a sense of a calm trust in Fate, even a submission to inevitable death. Yet courage on its own was frowned upon. It must be accompanied by honour. 'Death', says a Japanese writer on *bushido*, 'for a cause unworthy of dying was called a "dog's death".' A sense of shame was clearly part of this feeling for honour which the Japanese developed. The sword was called 'the soul of a samurai' and the act of *hara-kiri* became the outward expression of this feeling. A Japanese poem has the lines:

> 'When honour's lost, 'tis a relief to die;
> Death's but a sure retreat from infamy.'

Hara-kiri means literally 'ripping the belly', and we have on record a description of a famous ceremonial suicide and execution in a vast and imposing Japanese temple before seven Japanese and seven foreigners:

'Slowly and with great dignity the condemned man mounted onto the raised floor, lowered himself before the high altar twice and seated himself (in the Japanese fashion—knees and toes touching the ground and his body resting on his heels) on a felt carpet with his back to the altar. He took the wakizashi, a short sword or dirk of the Japanese, 9½ inches long with a point and edge as sharp as a razor's, and spoke, "I unwarrantably gave the order to fire on foreigners at Kobe; for this crime I disembowel myself." Deliberately, with a steady hand, he took the dirk and stabbed himself deeply below the waist in the left-hand side and drew the dirk slowly across to the right, and, turning it in the wound, gave a slight cut upward. During this sickeningly painful operation he never moved a muscle of his face. When he drew out the dirk he leaned forward stretching out his neck. At that moment the official executioner took a sword; then there was a flash, a heavy, ugly thud, a crashing fall; with one blow the head had been severed from the body.'

To the feudal samurai death in the service of one's lord was the final expression of loyalty, and this was the fourth feature of *bushido*. Over the centuries such loyalty became a religious cult for many who felt this was the way to salvation. The warrior's sense of loyalty and duty filtered through all Japanese society—lord and vassal, parents and children, husband and wife. It was a stern way of living. An old seventeenth-century document said, 'Avoid things that you like and turn your attention to unpleasant duties. Human life is like going on a long journey carrying a heavy load.'

The samurai was a man of action and his training was severe. It included fencing, archery and horsemanship as well as jiu-jitsu—the 'gentle art which uses no weapon'. Even low-ranking soldiers felt *bushido* was a noble ideal to work for. One such man wrote in a book entitled, *The Model Samurai*:

'When I was about sixteen I had a trend towards fatness. I had noticed a lack of agility in other fleshy persons and thought a heavy man would not make a first-class samurai. So I tried every means to keep myself agile and lean. I slept with my belt drawn tight and stopped eating rice; I drank no wine and avoided the company of women for the next ten years. When in my twenties I hardened myself by going into the fields on hot summer days and shooting skylarks, and in the winter months I spent several days in the mountains wearing only a cotton jacket over a cotton shirt. In such a way I disciplined myself.'

Modernization of the Army

Conscription was introduced into Japan in 1872. All men of twenty years were required to serve in the army for three years. This was the practical way in which loyalty to the State could be shown; but at the same time it destroyed the samurai as a separate class of professional soldiers. Resentment was widespread. A serious revolt broke out in 1877 in Satsuma led by a popular and respected man, Saigo, a samurai with all the *bushido* virtues—courage, generosity, swordsmanship and a well-known loyalty to his followers. It took six months and an army of 40,000 conscripted peasants to defeat Saigo. The commander of this army was Prince Yamagata.

Marshal the Prince Yamagata

A year later Yamagata reorganized the Japanese army on German lines. The German army had gained itself the reputation of being the world's most modern by defeating Austria and France within a space of five years. A Japanese General Staff was created which, like its German equivalent, would be responsible for planning the overall defence of the country; more reserves were established and new equipment brought in. All this cost money, and by 1890 one-third of the Japanese budget was being spent on the armed forces.

Yokohama jetty. Government troops embark to crush the Satsuma rebellion

Japan, with vigorous leadership and a speedy programme of modernization, had arrived at a point where she felt she could justifiably claim, as one Japanese put it, 'To rank equally with the other nations of the world'. Between 1890 and 1905 Japan became both feared and admired for her achievement, and thus gained her ambition—international recognition.

6 International Recognition

A Question of Pride and Status

Although Japan had made remarkable progress in modernization, one particular resentment became a main talking-point in the government. We saw in Chapter 3 that Japan in the 1850s had had to sign several treaties with different foreign powers, and that they were very one-sided. The system of extra-territoriality, which was a law by which foreigners living in Japan were outside the control of Japanese law courts, seemed to imply that the Japanese were not quite civilized. And only a 5 per cent tariff could be levied on imported goods, which certainly acted against Japan's domestic trading interests—she would have liked a much higher percentage to protect some of her infant industries against foreign competition. Revision of these 'unequal treaties' became a burning issue in Japan in the 1880s and '90s.

This resentment was mixed with other ambitions and fears. No Japanese wanted his country to become like China, where western powers had virtually taken over Chinese trade, so he was very suspicious of offers of foreign loans. Also, by 1890, Japan was facing a severe economic crisis. As industry grew the search for markets overseas for goods other than silk became vital. The country must export or go under said her businessmen, and they pointed to China as the most likely outlet. A great effort was made, and early in 1890 the Japanese Spinners' Association gained an important foothold in the Chinese market.

Some Japanese, however, were unwilling to wait for the traders. A patriotic society called the 'Genyosha' was formed to support an immediate expansion of Japanese influence and control onto the mainland—by armed force if necessary. The eyes of this society, which had the sympathy of the government, were fixed on Korea.

All these different pressures, diplomatic, commercial and expansionist, coincided in the year 1894, a key date in Japanese history. In that year long and difficult talks with the United States and Britain succeeded in abolishing the 'unequal treaties'. In that year also Japan went to war with China.

Victory and Humiliation

Korea was technically a state under Chinese influence. In the 1880s it opened, rather unwillingly, two ports to Japanese traders. The Chinese objected to this, but Viscount Ito, a very able Japanese diplomat, smoothed things over. In 1894 another crisis developed. Ito sent Japanese troops to take over the Korean Royal Palace when the Chinese began moving their own troops into the country. War followed and within a year

Marquis Ito the Japanese statesman

THE COREAN COCK-FIGHT.

Bruin. "HA!—WHICHEVER WINS, I SEE MY WAY TO A DINNER!"

Japan fights China in 1894 whilst Russia's Bruin looks greedily on

Japan had forced all Chinese troops out of Korea, taken control of the Yellow Sea, seized Port Arthur, and had seven divisions poised to move into China and capture Peking if necessary. Yamagata expressed the new Japanese military confidence: 'Our officers did not encounter any serious problems worthy of careful consideration.'

China sued for peace. By the Treaty of Shimonoseki in 1895, Japan gained Formosa, the key naval fortress of Port Arthur and its small peninsula, a large indemnity (money to pay for the war) from China, and Korea was recognized as 'independent', although clearly Japan intended keeping her influence there. The Japanese victory was so dramatic both by its speed

33

and by the value of the gains in the treaty that the rest of the world was astonished. Japan had taken a step towards achieving equal status with other world powers.

By showing herself to be a force to be reckoned with, however, she had created alarm amongst some powers. Within a week of the treaty of Shimonoseki being signed three European nations 'advised' Japan to return Port Arthur to China because, they said, Japanese possession of it 'would disturb the

JAP THE GIANT-KILLER.

How the British saw Japan's defeat of China in 1895

peace of the Far East'. Japan was in no position to resist this triple intervention by Russia, France and Germany, and Port Arthur was handed back.

This humiliation had deep effects on the Japanese. A mood of bitterness against western countries grew up. Nations Japan had once respected now became distrusted. Russia's intervention was soon revealed as two-faced, because in 1898 she received the lease of Port Arthur (that is the sole use of the port for Russian trade) from China. Japan's resentment

increased when a big 'scramble' for more concessions in China
followed.

Russia was Japan's main worry. In 1898 Russia had won the
right to construct a railway, the Chinese-Eastern, across the
Chinese territory of Manchuria to the Russian port of Vladivostock. This port, however, was ice-bound $3\frac{1}{2}$ months of the
year. Here was the explanation of Russia's interest in the ice-
free Port Arthur. By 1898 with this in her grasp Russia was in a
position to extend her control throughout Manchuria, and
possibly into north China and Korea. This Japan was determined to prevent.

The Anglo-Japanese Alliance

In 1900 the Boxer Rebellion occurred. Chinese patriots and
bandits, spurred on by the Boxer Society and its motto 'The
Fist of Concord and Justice', took over Peking. As a protest
against foreign influence in China they laid siege to the various
legations there in the city. Together with all the other western
powers except one, Japan sent in troops to restore order. The
exception was Russia. She used the disorder as an excuse to
occupy all Manchuria.

Japan was in a dilemma. She needed to preserve her trade
and markets on the mainland in order to keep up her prosperity at home. So she had either to bargain with Russia for a
share of her influence in Manchuria or to fight her. Ito led a
cautious group who thought the wisest course was negotiation,
and late in 1901 he went to Moscow to discuss things. Other
Japanese, led by Yamagata, looked to an alliance with Britain
as a preliminary to fighting Russia. The Triple Intervention of
1895 had convinced Japan that she must not enter another
conflict without an ally.

It was doubtful if Ito could have gained anything worthwhile from the Russians, but Britain feared he might. Anglo-
Russian relations had been poor for the last half century, as
Britain was suspicious of Russian expansion in the Balkan
region of Europe, to the north of India and in the Far East.
British trade with China was too valuable to allow Russian
interference. To many Japanese, Britain would be a more
reliable partner than Russia, so negotiations were opened. But
some delicate diplomacy was needed. Japan remembered

Punch magazine in London celebrates the Anglo-Japanese Alliance

ALLIES.

" Oh, East is East, and West is West . . . . . .
But there is neither East nor West, Border, nor Breed, nor Birth,
When two strong men stand face to face, tho' they come from the ends of the earth!"
—RUDYARD KIPLING.

Britain had not joined the Triple Intervention, and so many pro-British newspapers in Japan urged an agreement, but this was not a very solid basis on which to construct a serious international alliance. Much more important were two other factors. The first was the persistent efforts of Hayashi, the Japanese ambassador in London, who did the early sounding out; the second was the growing joint fear of Russian domination in the Korean and North China region.

An alliance was finally signed between Britain and Japan, on 30 January 1902, after some thorny questions had been solved. Britain for instance had no intention of getting involved in a private Russo-Japanese quarrel over Korea, and equally Japan did not want to send her troops as far as India to help Britain against possible Russian pressure there. India was eventually omitted from the terms, and careful wording of Korean references in the alliance document said Japan had interests in 'a peculiar degree politically' there. The real core of the Alliance said that if either Japan or Britain was attacked by *one* other country, the ally would remain neutral; but there would be mutual military aid if there were *two* or more aggressors.

Japan was jubilant. She was an equal partner with a nation which for a century had been the world's most powerful industrial and naval country. How would Russia react?

7 The Russo-Japanese War

The Origins of the War

The immediate consequence of the Anglo-Japanese Alliance was Russian alarm. Railways and battleships were the vital factors in international relations in the Far East at the beginning of the twentieth century. On both counts Russia saw an immediate contest with Japan would not be to her advantage. In 1902 her much-publicized Trans-Siberian Railway, which would supply her Far Eastern provinces, was a year short of completion; and her naval programme of building was just under way—she had now only two effective battleships to Japan's four.

So Russia back-pedalled. Within two months of the signing of the Anglo-Japanese Alliance, she began evacuating her troops from Manchuria. By a Chinese–Russian agreement this was to take place at six-month intervals.

Could Russia be trusted? In Japan two opposing points of view were discussed. Ito, as before, favoured negotiation. Russia must be persuaded to agree to free trading rights, or an 'open door' as it was called, in Manchuria and accept Japan's position in Korea. Yamagata thought this was wasting time. Japan, he said, would not have her naval superiority for ever and he demanded war. A compromise was reached. One last attempt would be made to make Russia see Japan's point of view, and Japanese diplomats left for St Petersburg. If they failed Japan would fight.

As it turned out, Russia had no intention of honouring even the six-month intervals of the agreement with China. The explanation of Russian policy, which seemed to take a zigzag course, was to be found in the bitter rivalry inside the Czar's court in St Petersburg. The Czar himself, Nicholas II, once admitted, 'I do not know anything regarding international

affairs', yet felt it his duty to carry the Russian flag into neighbouring countries. He was also impressed by Kaiser William
II's constant references to 'the Yellow Peril', which expressed
the fears that some Europeans had of the growing importance
and independence of some Asian countries. The ablest of
Nicholas's ministers was Sergei Witte, a clever, unscrupulous
figure who gave the sound advice in 1902 that war with Japan
would be disastrous. But a year later Witte resigned, giving
way to men with warlike, expansionist ideas. The evacuation
of Manchuria was halted and it was declared 'outside the
scope of the conversations' with the Japanese diplomats.

Port Arthur and Mukden

Japan did not wait any longer. The battleship 'race' had
already been reversed in Russian favour 7:6. On 9 February
1904 Japan launched a torpedo attack on Port Arthur, and
crippled two of Russia's biggest ships. The war that followed
had three phases: a long siege by the Japanese of Port Arthur;
the battle of Mukden; and the sea battle in the Straits of
Tsushima.

Both Japan and Russia faced serious problems. Japan had a
well-trained army, but the Port Arthur siege which cost

A Japanese cartoon showing Russia's Trans-Siberian Railway supplies crashing
through the ice of Lake Baikal

60,000 men drained that army of experienced officers. The Russians had the Trans-Siberian Railway, but it was single-track and had a hundred-mile gap at Lake Baikal, where supplies had to be hauled over the ice in winter. Given sufficient time the Russians could build up their army from enormous reserves in Europe. Japan dare not wait for this. Public and government opinion in Tokyo needed a spectacular victory with which to earn the respect and admiration of the world. However, General Nogi, commander of the Japanese army found the Russians strongly entrenched in the hills

Towards Port Arthur: planting the flag on the Liaotung Peninsula

around Port Arthur. He won through by dogged persistence only after five months, but at least destroyed the Russian threat to sea communications between Japan and the mainland.

Then early in 1905 Nogi led his army north for a decisive battle with the Russians—a third of a million of them massing near Mukden. In Manchuria the climate is extreme, with scorching summers and bitter winters, and valleys in which during winter 'the mud reaches the breasts of the horses', said a Russian officer. Open areas were covered by a tall grain, millet, ten to fifteen feet high, presenting great difficulties to infantry trying to manœuvre. In these conditions the Russians prepared to meet the army of a nation they despised. 'A Japanese', ran a Russian camp ditty, 'is nothing but a mosquito; we'll stick a pin in him and send him home in a letter.' But Russian leadership was poor. An observer commented, 'In Manchuria every army chief waited inactive until his neighbour was defeated, in order to have a justification for his own retreat under the pretext of straightening the line'. Nogi conducted a hustling offensive around Mukden for three weeks in the hope of drawing the Russians into a major battle. But they withdrew their remnants into Siberia to regroup. The tired Japanese army could claim success, although spectacular victory seemed as elusive as ever.

Tsushima

For many months it had been recognized that naval power would be the decisive factor in the war. In order to keep control of Manchuria Russia must destroy Japanese command of the sea. So late in 1904 a Russian fleet of forty vessels set out from their home base in the Baltic Sea to sail half way round the world to Vladivostock. They included four battleships which had not yet had their maiden voyages, and the crews of which were so lacking in training that they could not even shoot at a target effectively. Six months later this fleet arrived in the Sea of Japan. The Japanese navy, with ships built largely in British yards and officers professionally trained by the British, was well aware of the importance of its task. Its commander was Admiral Togo, one of the great heroic figures of Japanese history. A war correspondent described him as having, 'a pleasant face, bright eyes and a fine nose, with a

To Vladivostock

✕ Russian surrender

KOREA

Night of
May 27th/28th

Admiral
Togo's
route

Port Mason

2 p.m.
✕ 27th May
1905

HONSHU

Tsushima
Is.

Straits of Tsushima

SHIKOKU

SHIKOKU

KYUSHU

Russian Fleet

The Battle of Tsushima. (Port Arthur is off the map about 300 miles along the west
Korean coast)

sparse beard turning gray at the chin'. To his fleet Togo
delivered the following message, which was meant to be a
paraphrase of Nelson's at Trafalgar: 'The country's fate
depends upon this battle. Let every man do his duty with all
his might.'

The comparison with Trafalgar was taken a stage further
when, between two and three o'clock in the afternoon of
27 May 1905, the Japanese gained the overwhelming victory
they had been seeking for so long. Togo, depending on Russian
inefficiency and slowness and on his own new armour-piercing
shells, manœuvred his fleet with great courage and order right
under the noses of the Russians. Then as the commander of a
Russian battleship wrote later, 'Shells seemed to rain down

upon us without pause; the high temperature of the explosive spread a kind of liquid fire which smothered everything.' For the loss of 3 small torpedo boats and 117 men Togo destroyed the Russian fleet at Tsushima. 4,830 Russians died in the Sea of Japan and only 2 ships made Vladivostock harbour.

The Peace of Portsmouth

Russia faced serious unrest at home; Japan was in financial difficulties. Both countries therefore accepted American mediation, and at Portsmouth, in the state of New Hampshire, U.S.A., a treaty was drawn up in September 1905. Japan demanded railway rights in Manchuria, Port Arthur, the southern end of Sakhalin, a large indemnity and Russian recognition of Japan's interests in Korea. Although the Russians refused to pay an indemnity, they gave way on all the other points. Knowing how close their country was to financial exhaustion the Japanese diplomats agreed to the modified treaty. The ordinary people in Tokyo rioted when it became obvious that without an indemnity Japanese taxes would have to go up to pay for the war.

However, Japan had benefited enormously both in the extension of her influence on the mainland and in prestige. Within a dozen years she had ended the 'unequal treaties', allied on equal terms with one major European power and successfully challenged and defeated another. The ghost of Commodore Perry had been laid.

8 Ambition beyond Reason

The Twenty-One Demands 1915

Japan owed her rapid rise in power and international status to three things: the ability of her statesmen, a new conscript army trained in Bushido ideals, and the energy and industrial skill of her people. How would she use this power? With Korea and southern Manchuria firmly under her influence, Japan was ready to extend her commercial interests in China on a large scale. She wanted in fact to do what western countries had been doing for many years. 1915 was the year of opportunity.

When the First World War broke out in 1914 Japan had joined Britain according to the terms of the Anglo-Japanese Alliance. She quickly dealt with German possessions in the Pacific area, among them Shantung and its port of Tsingtao. This was just the other side of the Yellow Sea from Port Arthur and, with Shantung in her control, Japan saw a chance to get big concessions from China. In 1915 Premier Okuma and Foreign Minister Kato presented a set of twenty-one demands to China. The most important required that China must agree to Japanese presence in Shantung and grant extra commercial privileges in Manchuria; China was not to lease any more coastal territory to other powers; and lastly China was to accept political, financial and military advisers sent from Japan. After long talks and much pressure China gave in to all except the last demand. Okuma and Kato felt they had good reason to be satisfied.

The plan soon went wrong. Many Japanese felt they had the right, the ability and the determination to be undisputed masters of eastern Asia, but quarrels developed in the government over the methods to be used. Yamagata, for instance, opposed Kato's bullying of China because it aroused too much hostility in China and among the western powers. His argument was supported by Japanese traders who found the Twenty-one Demands destroyed much of the goodwill they had carefully built up in previous years.

Abroad the Demands and the general expansionist trends of Japanese policy aroused suspicion and fear. They were to prove the turning-point in American–Japanese relations. In 1905 the United States had seen 'a Gallant Little Japan whip the Russian Bear'. In 1915 this image changed to 'the Bully in China'.

The Siberian Expedition

Late in 1917 the Bolshevik Revolution took place in European Russia. Lenin immediately opened peace talks with the Germans, but faced a civil war against a variety of anti-Bolshevik forces. In the Far East Japan thought it could profit out of the confusion. Particularly, senior Japanese army officers feared any extension of Bolshevik revolutionary ideas to Manchuria, Korea and China, and so they planned a big military operation in the Russian Far Eastern provinces.

The Japanese government could not at first get British and American (Japan's allies against Germany) agreement to this —until in the summer of 1918 Czech prisoners, having escaped from Russian camps, organized themselves into an army, and fought their way to the Pacific coast and seized Vladivostock. The Americans, although they were still suspicious, agreed to let the Japanese government send 'an army division only' to support the Czechs. Matters soon got out of hand. The single division became five, and the Japanese army mopped up all Siberia as far as Lake Baikal! The Siberian 'intervention' became an army affair with the government at home exercising little control. The cost of keeping 70,000 soldiers there rose rapidly, however, and Japan's position became very difficult in the next few years. At the end of the First World War the few British and American troops withdrew, and by 1921 the Bolsheviks had re-established themselves in Siberia. Japan withdrew in 1922, humiliated.

The Siberian Expedition left a painful legacy. Abroad mistrust of Japan grew—there was a general feeling that her ambitions were becoming selfish and uncontrollable. At home severe attacks were made on the government because of the cost, the loss of prestige and particularly failure to control the army.

The Washington Conference

The Twenty-One Demands and the Siberian affair had strained American–Japanese relations considerably. A third issue nearly produced war. In the Pacific a naval armaments race was developing among the major powers. In an effort to prevent conflict a conference of interested nations met in Washington in 1921. After some hard bargaining three agreements were made. The Anglo-Japanese Alliance, which for Britain had served its purpose, was replaced by a new, rather vague pact between Britain, France, America and Japan, who said they would 'respect each other's rights' in the Pacific area. On the question of naval armaments Japan reluctantly agreed that a 5:5:3 ratio in warship tonnage should be established for Britain, the United States and Japan respectively. Finally, Japan was pressed to withdraw her troops from Shantung.

The Price of Ambition

By 1922 it was clear that Japan's ambitions on the Asiatic mainland had gone far beyond what she could reasonably hope to administer efficiently *and* what the other world powers would tolerate. By over-reaching herself in China and Siberia Japan had created suspicion of her future intentions. So far she had gained little direct profit and no glory from her expansionist policy.

Liberal-minded Japanese, however, who were concerned about their country's reputation throughout the world, were worried about two dangerous developments. In Siberia the army had 'gone it alone' and paid no attention to orders from the government in Tokyo. There was also noisy criticism of the government's 'weak-kneed China policy' from extrem groups called ultra-nationalists, who urged the continued expansion of Japanese power in Asia. One of these groups, the Black Dragon Society, had close relations with the militarists in Japan's army.

9 The 'Twenties: Japan in Difficulties

Weak Governments

After the First World War Japan, in common with many other industrialized nations, suffered from the extremes of trade boom and depression. She had a short period of prosperity during and just after the war when there was a great demand for her goods, but this gradually dried up as European countries recovered from the devastation and began competing again with Japan. Other problems too made the early 1920s a difficult period for the Japanese. There was a rapidly rising population, a terrible earthquake and an emigration crisis with the United States.

To solve all these problems firm leadership in the government was necessary. But nearly all the statesmen who had led Japan's modernization were dead—Ito in 1909, Nogi in 1912 and in 1922 Yamagata died. There were few men of ability among their successors. An attempt to bring democracy and liberal ideas to Japan also petered out. The elected representatives of the people (all men over twenty-five were given the vote in 1925) seemed irresponsible. One observer wrote of the members of Japan's parliament: 'Warmed within by too copious draughts of saké (rice wine), they roared and bellowed; and arguments frequently culminated in a rush for the rostrum, whence the speaker of the moment would be dragged into a free fight.'

Bribery was common and it became well known that the massive *zaibatsu* industrial combines used their influence to get the best government contracts. There was little respect for such a parliament and government from the Japanese people as a whole.

48

The Rice Riots of 1918

The boom in trade during the First World War had caused prices to rise. This is called inflation, and it affected the price of rice, Japan's staple or main food. The peasants who produced the rice could demand good prices for it; but the poorer-paid urban worker who had to buy it found great hardship. Spontaneous rioting took place in the cities of Japan in August 1918, Osaka and Kobe suffering the worst. The anger of the rioters was directed against the wartime profiteers whose shop-windows were smashed and cars overturned and burnt. Troops were eventually brought in to keep law and order. There was a good deal of grumbling, however, from shop-keepers and property-owners about how slow the authorities had been to take action.

Moga and Mobo

Another feature of Japanese society in the 'twenties disturbed the more conservative people. This was the *Moga* style of behaviour and living. *Moga* was an abbreviation of *modan garu*, the Japanese words for 'modern girl', and *Mobo* was the 'modern boy' equivalent. They adopted dress fashions of the western world, especially those of the younger generation: cloche hats, short skirts, the shingle or Eton crop hairstyle for girls, and showy western jackets and trousers, like the Oxford bags, for the young men. In traditional Japanese society these trends were frowned upon. To many of the older generation they were symbols of the break-up of an accepted way of life. Hostility to things western began replacing the frenzied 'westernization' we saw in Chapter 4. People with influence suggested that Japan turn away from the West entirely, and their views found support in places like the Black Dragon Society and the army.

The Great Earthquake of 1923

At two minutes to noon on 1 September 1923 an earthquake rippled in spasms along the Tokyo–Yokohama Plain. An eye-witness compared it to 'a carpet with a draught under it'. At the Tokyo Seismological Institute, where earth tremors are studied, experts calculated that the epicentre, or starting-point, of the earthquake was over sixty miles to the south of the

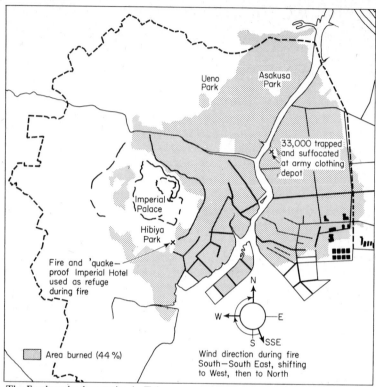

The Earthquake devastation in Tokyo 1923

capital. The tremor began slowly, took twelve seconds to reach its peak and held it for another five seconds. The concrete and brick walls of the Institute 'were shaking to an extraordinary extent and tiles were showering down'. Within two minutes all was over.

Japan has several hundred earth tremors a year, though only a few cause serious damage. As had happened before after an earthquake, tidal waves wrecked coastal resorts and inland the flimsy walls of the average Japanese home, made of sliding wood panels, crumpled. But this time circumstances were exceptional, and the 1923 'quake proved the most devastating in recorded Japanese history. The day was hot and a high wind was blowing. Large numbers of Tokyo's citizens were cooking their lunchtime rice over charcoal braziers. When the tremors began there was a rush for the streets. Then the 'Flowers of Yedo' took hold; this was the local name for earthquake fires. Wood crashing onto braziers, smashed gas-mains and the strong wind turned Tokyo into a furnace. People crowded the bridges and open spaces, but could not get away from the sparks and hot ash. In one such place in a poor part of the city 30,000 died. Altogether 107,000 people died and two-thirds of Tokyo lay in ruins.

Nearer the epicentre, nothing was saved in Yokohama. The heat was so fierce that living trees blazed like matchwood and small rivers, into which people jumped for safety, evaporated.

In both Tokyo and Yokohama the final devastation came in the afternoon. Immense heat at ground-level burnt up the air and caused more air to rush in to replace it. Scores of small but violent whirlwinds, resembling the swirling, funnel-shapes of tornadoes, ripped apart any solid building still erect. One of

A postman's problems: finding the address for letters after the 1923 earthquake

the landmarks of Tokyo, a twelve-storey block of flats, collapsed in rubble when one of these 'dragons' tails' caught it.

Next day the looting began. The savagery of the bewildered
and homeless reached a climax when the mob, searching for
someone to blame, found a scapegoat—the Korean immigrants. Wild rumours spread that nationalists from Korea had
tried to use the earthquake as a cover for setting up a revolutionary government. In the ugly riots which followed 4,000
Koreans were murdered by gangs of 'patriotic' Japanese
youths.

1923 is a year the Japanese prefer to forget . . .

Immigration Quotas

In the 'twenties Japan's relations with America continued to
get worse. The Japanese particularly objected to the 'lectur-
ing' tone of United States diplomatic letters and the editorials
of some American newspapers. Who were the Americans to
preach to Japan about the Siberian Expedition, for instance,
and on the rights and wrongs of international behaviour? The
Japanese accused the Americans of hypocrisy. 'You are only
trying to keep your valuable Chinese trade to yourself', cried
the Tokyo press.

The arguments so far—the Twenty-One Demands, Siberia
and naval rivalry—were mainly government matters, but a
fourth issue touched the ordinary Japanese very closely. It was
the question of Japanese immigration into the United States,
especially California, and it raised fierce passions on both sides.

Until the turn of the century there had been hardly any
Japanese in America; then in 1900 12,000 entered in the hope
of better wages. California reacted immediately. Congress in
1901 heard senators call the Japanese a 'menace to the industrial interests of our people'. By 1906 an Exclusion League
had been set up in San Francisco with the slogan, 'California
is a White Man's Country'. The American government in
Washington at first refused to support such an attitude, but by
the end of the First World War pressure was brought to bear
from such societies as 'The Native Sons and Daughters of the
Golden West'.

The Japanese regarded all this with distaste. Then two
events destroyed what little goodwill still existed between the

two countries. In 1919, at the Versailles Peace Conference which followed the War, Japan proposed that the principle of racial equality be included in the League of Nations declaration. The idea had a stormy reception. President Wilson of the United States was in favour until he was warned of possible rioting in California, where the principle clashed with the State laws excluding Japanese immigrants from owning land. Hughes of Australia, an unyielding supporter of the White Australia Policy (deliberately aimed at keeping coloured Asiatics out of the country), and called by a British statesman 'an inveterate trouble-maker' drove hard at this weakness in the American front. As a result the idea was not accepted.

Five years later a bill was introduced in the United States Congress limiting immigration from all countries to 150,000 persons a year, and excluding specifically 'Asiatics' from such a quota. There had been several clashes between 'whites' and 'yellows' on big Californian farms where Japanese labour was blamed for wage-cuts. The bill was passed. San Francisco had won.

On 15 April 1924 Tokyo newspapers lashed out at the United States for 'this grave insult' and 'this deliberate slap in the face'. An expert on Japanese affairs has commented, 'The hurt to Japanese pride was deep and long-lasting'. The immigration crisis played straight into the hands of the anti-western and militarist groups in Japan. Must Japan, they argued, continue to kow-tow to those who despised her?

1929–31 The Great Depression

Many of these difficulties facing Japan in the 1920s arose from a kind of split personality. Along with Western powers like Britain, the United States, Australia, New Zealand, France and Holland, Japan had trading rights in China and colonies scattered over the Far East. Because of this she felt she belonged to a world-wide 'club' of important and powerful countries. Yet many Japanese could not really forget that they were Asiatics. Much of their long history was closely linked with the mainland of Asia, and they saw themselves in a way as spokesmen for the peoples of that continent in the racial equality issue of 1919.

Another reason for Japan's difficulties was the fear and

resentment abroad of some features of her industrial revolution. A world trading boom in the early twentieth century had given Japan the chance of becoming a leading producer of cotton goods, toys and pottery. Cheap wares with 'Made in Japan' stamped on them were a familiar sight in the bazaars of the Far East and on the Woolworth's '3*d* and 6*d*' counters of the United States and Europe. During the Great Depression of 1929–31, when millions throughout the world became unemployed, many protests were made about these shoddy Japanese goods, which were undercutting western products. Tariffs (high import duties) were put on Japanese articles in an effort to keep them from competing with European and American manufactures.

The following figures show the prices Japanese traders could get for their raw silk, still an important export. (This table is called a Price Index as it is based on 100, and a comparison can be made from year to year.)

```
1914: 100
1925: 222
1929: 151
1931:  67
```

In one Japanese town alone investigations showed that, in 1930, 22,000 silk-reeling girls had not been paid for months. They continued to work, finding it better to receive food and shelter than nothing at all.

The Japanese army found the distressed areas an easy recruiting ground. The army also thought it had a practical answer to Japan's difficulties: action in Manchuria.

Many soldiers came from the countryside. Before we see them at war, let us take a brief glance at rural life as they knew it.

10   Interlude: Rural Japan in the 1930s

In the far south-west of Japan there is a small village, Suye Mura. In 1935 John Embree went to live there for six months, and wrote a remarkably vivid and detailed study of the life and environment of a Japanese peasant in the period between the two world wars.

The House

Houses were usually single-storey thatched cottages, with walls of wood-and-paper sliding screens and a little mud wattle. Outside doors were rarely closed: even if the whole family was out in the fields, a visitor would never think of entering unless someone were there to receive him. There were usually three living and sleeping rooms divided by sliding panels: the main living space, with a fire-pit in the centre; the 'best' room which had the finest mats and two alcoves for family treasures and religious ornaments; and a third area was partitioned for sleeping the children, the grandparents, sons- and daughters-in-law. The master and his wife would sleep in the best room. Everyone used the floor to eat and sleep on as there was very little furniture, though guests would be given thin, square cushions to kneel on.

The diagram on page 56 shows the general layout—there is a kitchen marked, but it had a dirt floor and its roof was only a lean-to, and so the room was not regarded as part of the house proper.

The floors of the house were covered with *tatami* mats, which were a feature of most Japanese households in both town and country, and still are today. They are made of rice straw, $1\frac{1}{2}$ inches thick, covered with a woven rush of better quality and hemmed with cloth. *Tatami* measure about six feet by three feet, and Japanese rooms are sized accordingly: $4\frac{1}{2}$, 6, 8 *tatami* mats. The covering is smooth and hard-wearing, and a

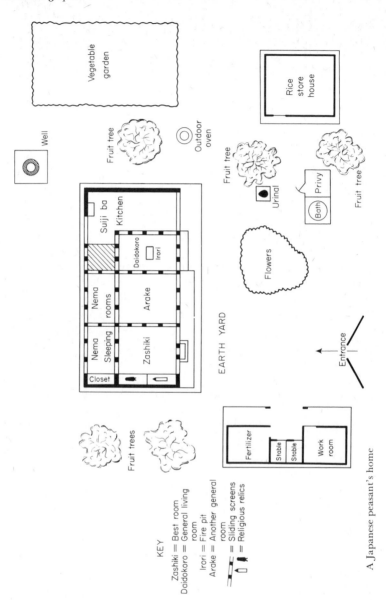

KEY

Zashiki = Best room
Daidokoro = General living
room
Irori = Fire pit
Arake = Another general
room
= Sliding screens
= Religious relics

A Japanese peasant's home

new *tatami* would be springy and quite pleasant to sit on, especially in hot weather.

Mother pounding millet in the yard while the children play

Just outside the house was an area of bare flat earth where the rice plants were dried in the sun, and where in the slack farming season a man made baskets and his wife reeled silk.

Family Ties

In Japanese society close family relations have always been of prime importance, and in rural Japan the farmer's home would be the centre of family life. The entire household lived together here. It was made up of master, wife, all unmarried children and the eldest son's wife and family. 'Sons' could be and were often adopted (especially nephews), for great importance and prestige were attached to continuing the family name.

Within the family the master's decision was law, and he took precedence in all things. He was the first to take a bath, first to be served with food and had a special place to sit; all the farm's income went to the master and the wife was given money for household expenses only as she needed it. It was

57

perhaps the most important characteristic of life on a peasant farm that everyone worked not for himself but for the household.

The regular evening bath had an important social significance, especially for the women. Well-water was heated by firewood around 5 p.m. The work was so hard and cost of firewood so high that three or four households would work in rotation to provide the bath. Japanese women had little status in the rural home, and the social gathering for a bathe allowed strong ties of affection to develop between the women and children of neighbouring households; this was for some women their only social contact outside their own family.

Family togetherness did not exist outside the home. So much was it felt that a woman's place was in the home that man and wife would never be seen walking out in the street together; even brother and sister would only make rare appearances with each other.

The basic dress was the kimono, a wrap-around garment held together by a cloth belt. Varieties of design and shape were used for work, parties, in winter and summer, by young and old, men and women. In the 1930s western-style clothing was only just beginning to reach the villages of Japan.

Rice was the main crop and chief source of income for most of the families in the village. It was the staple food, usually in a boiled form, although sweets and cakes were often made with rice as the main ingredient. A man would eat two to three large bowls full each meal. Rice, in the remote rural areas like Suye Mura, was still used widely for money, and the value attached to it was shown by the fact that it was the only thing regularly locked up.

There were two traditional Japanese religious faiths, Buddhism and Shinto. (Shinto was a mixture of nature-worship and ancestor-worship.) Although a peasant did not understand theology, small relics always had a prominent place on an alcove shelf in his home. There was not much formal religion. In other words the villager did not often attend a shrine or temple, for it was believed that the priests had a duty to 'represent' the peasant in his worship. But the peasant hoped that Buddha would save his soul after death, while the many Shinto gods protected him during his life.

A Shinto priest

School

Before he went to school a Japanese child in this village was very spoiled. There was no discipline and if he cried for anything persistently he was given it. It was common to hear an angry youngster hitting out at his mother and crying *baka* (meaning 'fool').

But during his six years of schooling a boy entered a very different world. It was a harsh, rigidly organized life. The

59

school building was a long wooden hut with no heating—it was a traditional Japanese belief that discomfort was good for learning. Should a child complain, his teacher reminded him of the brave Japanese soldiers who had been in Siberia or who guarded the railway lines of Manchuria, 'where it is really cold!'

Many hours were spent learning how to read and write, but school always began at 7.50 a.m. with physical exercises performed to a government-controlled broadcast. Then the six-year-olds had singing. Nursery rhymes about birds and insects were chanted alongside verses with patriotic lines like, 'The beautiful national flag with the red sun on it' and:

'With his gun over his shoulder the soldier marches;
To the sound of the bugle he marches,
The beautiful soldier; I love the soldier.'

Older boys were occasionally sent to the nearby town school for lectures on the Japanese 'spirit', and second sons were encouraged to emigrate to Manchuria.

Acceptance without question of everything a teacher said at school was the rule. By the time they had completed their schooling Japanese boys and girls had become not only literate, but had also absorbed many ideas about patriotic duty and Japan's military spirit.

Growing up and Marriage Problems

Apart from the children of the few better-off villagers, who went to a high school, at fourteen years a boy was taking his full share in the farm work alongside his parents and sisters. There was scant time for romance for the adolescent during the long hours spent in the mud of the paddy fields or in the heavy work of collecting firewood. He would hear tales from the older generation of their secret love-affairs. These were a common feature of rural life before the First World War and they were helped by the absence of any light on the dark evenings (candles and paraffin were expensive and a fire hazard) and by the easy entry into Japanese houses by the sliding doors.

However, by the 1930s such behaviour by the younger generation was becoming more difficult—if not less common!

Part of Suye Mura—the rice harvest is being gathered

Many peasant homes had electric light which, because it was paid for by the number and wattage of the bulbs and not by kilowatt hours, was often left on all night. Love matches were, in any case, rare. Marriage in rural areas was a matter of 'arrangement' between two families. Only if violent disapproval was expressed by the young man (he would be about twenty-four) or by the girl (she would be about eighteen) was the match dropped.

At first a 'marriage' was merely a family matter. Using a go-between, the heads of the two families arranged the ceremony. The main part of this was the journey of the bride from her parental home to her in-laws' home, where an exchange of wine-cups and the feasting of relatives and the go-between completed the ritual. Only later, when a child was born, was the marriage likely to be recorded in the village records office.

Until then there was always a chance that the 'marriage' would break up. The wife had to accept without question the orders of her mother-in-law, because this was thought to be vital in training the wife to the ways of her new family. Divorce was quite common. The head of the family simply drew up a document called a 'divorce bill', beginning, 'It is our pleasure to divorce . . .' followed by the reason. The wife

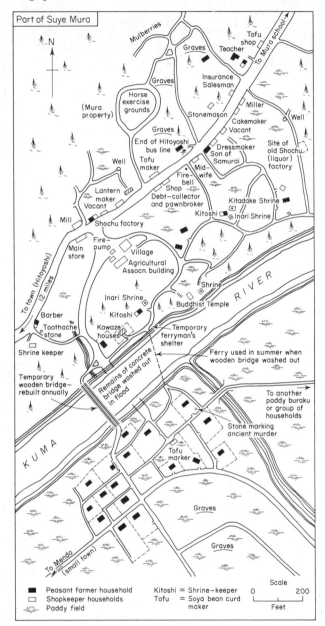

Suye Mura. Most of the village is shown here

then returned to her own family. A common explanation in old Japan was that 'the wife does not fit into the ways of the family', which probably meant she had quarrelled with her mother-in-law.

In a way of life where a girl had hardly any say in the choice of husband and her importance was limited to managing the household, she was expected to be a dutiful wife. Occasionally she became awkward and unco-operative, but such behaviour made her unpopular in the village where sly hints were made that she was a sorceress or witch. But in general a girl accepted that she had married for family reasons: to have children, mend clothes and cook food.

Because a farmer's wife also shared in the farm work an affectionate relationship might develop between man and wife. Other villagers, like the shopkeepers, often found they lacked such companionship, so these men went occasionally to the neighbouring town. Here they visited the geisha house for some relaxation with women highly-trained in singing, dancing and providing interesting conversation.

For a young man a year in the army might be part of the growing-up process. Once a year an army officer came to Suye Mura to conscript the twenty-year-olds. A brief medical check was followed by a longer talk on patriotism. About a third of the local men would pass the officer's inspection, and, although conscription normally only meant twelve months in a barracks in Japan, those chosen were given large send-off parties.

Forces bringing Change

John Embree found that the pattern of life in the remoter Japanese villages was an old one, probably dating back to medieval times. What you have read so far shows that this old pattern was based on two things: rice cultivation and the close co-operation both within and between families.

But Embree also found that the influence of western ideas and the control of the government in Tokyo were breaking down some of these patterns. For instance, as the use of cash in the village became more common, so the willing co-operation between families lessened. Forty years previously money had been used for only 10 per cent of a household's living needs. Now in the 1930s the percentage had risen to fifty. Cash was used in the shops of Suye Mura for tobacco, medicines, sugar, salt, fabrics and shoes.

As we have seen, the kerosene lamp was giving way to electricity, and out in the fields new machinery, artificial fertilizers, and winter wheat showed that other changes were taking place.

The newspapers were giving the peasants a wider view of the world, and the bicycle and bus brought a regular contact with the nearby towns. And although he did not understand much about national politics, a peasant took a certain pride in using his vote on election day.

Suye Mura in the period between the wars was changing slowly. The family, the household and village co-operation were still important features of life there. But all the changes seemed to emphasize that an individual also mattered—that young men should make their own way in the world by their own efforts.

Suye Mura villagers co-operate in bridge building with straw, bamboo and vines

Movement to the Towns

Because of the small size of the peasant farm holdings many of the older children left the village to find work in the expanding towns. There was an enormous city growth in Japan from 1935–40 when rapid industrialization demanded a huge labour force. In the towns work could be found either in the small workshops with between five and fifty employees, or in the *zaibatsu*-controlled industrial combines like Mitsubishi and Mitsui which could provide jobs in a wider field: railways, ships, coal and electricity power, banking and insurance. Japan's industrial progress in the twentieth century was very much due to the efforts of these small and big employers alike. They 'got things done'.

This progress was achieved at great human cost. Peasant daughters who went to the towns found they had to accept iron discipline and long hours. A 'dormitory' system grew up in which young girls aged fourteen to twenty were hired on a contract basis for three years. They were then housed, fed and largely confined to the factory premises where they worked. The government hardly ever enquired into their welfare, and 'sweatshop' conditions, child labour, widespread tuberculosis and a high accident rate became common features of Japanese urban life in the 1930s.

The movement from the rural areas continued. Whatever might be thought of the living standards in the towns, which were low compared with the western world, Japan had a better standard than other Asiatic countries. This was shown in the expectation of life figures. A Japanese boy born in 1935 could expect to live ten years longer than his grandfather, born in the 1880s, and twenty years longer than a Chinese boy born also in 1935.

11　The Manchurian Incident 1931

The Kwantung Army Plan

Ever since the Russo-Japanese War and the Twenty-One Demands Japan had slowly been extending her influence in Manchuria. Territorially she controlled Port Arthur and the railway line running north beyond Mukden. In terms of economic wealth, investments in coal and iron, salt, the distillation of oil-shale and soya-bean cultivation meant also that important Japanese interests must be safeguarded. Japan claimed that Manchuria had always been a kind of no-man's-land, and in the war of 1904–5 she had 'saved Manchuria from Russia'. The Chinese refused to accept this situation, and they wanted to squeeze Japan out of the area little by little. To protect her interests Japan had a small army in the Port Arthur region called the Kwantung Army. Officers of this army were convinced that Japan ought to seize all Manchuria before it was too late.

Sporadic violence in Manchuria in the summer of 1931 gave colour to the army's case. A Japanese intelligence officer was murdered in June. Then some fighting in July about an irrigation ditch between some Chinese farmers and Korean settlers was stopped when Japanese army police took the Koreans' side. Rumours of widespread persecution of other Koreans by the Chinese reached Pyongyang, the chief town of north Korea. Here Chinese residents were attacked, a hundred killed and houses were looted and burned.

In Tokyo officers of the General Staff demanded extra money in the army budget so that more troops could be sent to Manchuria. The Japanese Cabinet, led by the Foreign Minister, Shidehara, opposed this. Shidehara's policy was one of friendly co-operation with China, and instead of granting the money he threatened to cut down the budget, and even offered compensation to China for the Pyongyang 'massacre'. The Kwantung Army officers were particularly irritated at Shidehara's 'weak diplomacy', because they were in the process of drawing up a plan to seize control of key points in Manchuria.

Diary of an Incident

Even today no one knows how much of this plan was known in Tokyo, but reliable reports of 'something in the wind' reached Shidehara. He advised the Emperor who issued a command that the army should restrain itself.

It was too late.

A letter was sent to the Commander-in-Chief of the Kwantung Army ordering him to cancel any military plans against the Chinese. The major-general chosen for the delivery of this letter was a secret sympathizer with the Kwantung Army's plan, and he deliberately made slow progress to the army headquarters near Mukden. Even so he arrived a few hours before he knew action was planned, and with the letter still in his pocket he visited a local tea-house, which was used as a sort of social club by the officers. Whilst there, on the evening

Japanese soldiers in a Mukden street in 1931

of 18 September, the 'Manchurian Incident' took place. The following timetable shows how quickly events moved:

18 SEPT. 1931

10.30 p.m.	A Japanese army patrol is marching along the main line of the South Manchurian Railway, near Mukden. There is an explosion behind them. On investigation some railway sleepers are found damaged. A few Chinese soldiers are seen running away: three are killed. (This was the official Japanese army statement; its truth has never been proved.)

19 SEPT. 1931

2.20 a.m.	All Japanese troops in the Mukden area are mobilized; the town arsenal and aerodrome are seized.
4.30 a.m.	Mukden's local radio station is captured.
Dawn	All Mukden is in Japanese hands.
Breakfast-time	In Tokyo, Shidehara is told of these events. Reporters say, 'his face turned grey'.
10.00 a.m.	Cabinet meets in Tokyo. Minister of War states: 'I am anxious that Japanese residents on the mainland should not be exposed to persecution; more troops must be sent to Manchuria.' Shidehara is severely criticized for his weak policy. He wavers and says, 'I hope the Incident will soon be closed.'

20 SEPT. 1931

China appeals to the League of Nations. Cabinet meets in Tokyo again. The Minister of War urges an extension of military operations 'to ensure a Japanese victory'; the Finance Minister protests at 'the waste of money'; Shidehara fears 'foreign complications'.

22 SEPT. 1931
The League of Nations meets in Geneva. The
Japanese delegate says, 'the trouble is due to
some military hot-heads; the best thing is to
do nothing until better minds are in control
again'.

30 SEPT. 1931
League demands that Japanese troops in
Manchuria withdraw to their original
territory. The Japanese delegate accepts this
proposal.

BUT: SEPTEMBER TO DECEMBER 1931

Kwantung Army occupies all Manchuria.
The Chinese withdraw south of the Great
Wall of China.

As the Japanese saw it: their photographic evidence of the blown Mukden railway line

THE HANDS OF THE LEAGUE;
OR, HER FIRST GREAT TEST.

The League of Nations tries to solve the 'Manchurian Incident' 1931

Consequences

The contrast between what the government of Japan was
saying and what its Army in Manchuria was actually doing led
the rest of the world, and particularly the League of Nations,
to denounce the Japanese Cabinet as a bunch of hypocrites.
But in fact, as one senior Japanese officer said later, 'From the
beginning to the end the government has been utterly fooled
by the army'. An American correspondent echoed this when

he wrote to his paper, 'The Foreign Office had been tied to the chariot wheels of war.'

The Japanese newspapers came out strongly in favour of the action of the Kwantung Army, and membership of ultra-nationalist groups like the Black Dragon Society increased. It became dangerous to criticize the Manchurian Incident in public.

In 1932 the League of Nations sent an investigation team to Manchuria. Its leader was Britain's Lord Lytton, and in September it issued a report condemning Japan, who as a result quit the League in February 1933. No further efforts were made to control Japan, but the use of force to gain her ambitions put her, in the minds of many people abroad, into the same 'bloc' as Mussolini's Italy and the new Nazi-controlled Germany. The Manchurian affair did considerable damage to the chances of keeping world peace in the difficult 1930s, when dictators in Europe found building up an army was one way to solve unemployment problems.

12 Government by Assassination

Unrest at Home

The Japanese tried to put a united front to the rest of the world during the Manchurian crisis, but at home different points of view clashed and could barely be concealed. The central problem was the power of the army. Two developments in 1932 showed an increase in the army's confidence.

An independent government was set up in Manchuria. The new state was to be called Manchukuo and its ruler the last of the Chinese emperors of the Manchu Dynasty, Pu Yi, who had been overthrown in a revolution in 1911–12. However, the Commander-in-Chief of the Kwantung Army was appointed Japanese ambassador, and it was clear to everybody that Pu Yi was merely a puppet and Manchukuo a kind of private empire of the Japanese Army.

Also in 1932 fighting broke out in the great commercial port of Shanghai between Chinese soldiers and a Japanese naval party attached to the international trading quarter of the city. In six weeks of bloodthirsty clashes Japan committed four army divisions to rescue the small naval force.

As a result of these episodes the army's prestige rose and that of the 'civilian' power in Tokyo declined. However, there was not only a gulf between the army and the politicians; the army itself had problems. Two groups within the officer corps vied with each other for power. One was called 'The Imperial Way Group'. It had many junior officers among its supporters, and favoured a struggle with Russia on the mainland, that is Japanese expansion northwards from Manchuria. The other was 'The Control Group', which thought Japan should move southwards against China, at the same time establishing good relations with the Soviet Union.

The Assassination Plots of 1932

As part of this internal contest for power in Japan, three major assassination plots occurred between 1932 and 1936. Ultra-nationalist fanatics of the Black Dragon type of society played an important part in such plots, whilst two closely involved the military. A would-be assassin followed a code of conduct expressed some years before:

'A word to my colleagues. Do not be conspicuous. You must be quiet and simply stab, cut, stick and shoot. Just sacrifice your life. Just die, just sleep.'

The cult of patriotism had become separated from reason and morality. One fanatic, Kita Ikki, had written a kind of bible for 'patriots'. In order to make Japan fit for the leadership of Asia, he argued, a clean sweep of the country's present politicians was necessary.

Early in 1932 an ex-finance minister who had spoken against an increase in the army's budget was shot by a member of 'The League of Blood'. And within a month Baron Dan of the Mitsui Company was murdered because he was suspected of corruption.

Then came the May Plot against the Prime Minister and his government. Nine young naval and army officers, equipped with revolvers and hand-grenades, entered the Premier's home. But their preparations had been very amateurish: they lost their way in the house, and only by luck found the Premier whom they shot. They panicked and fled, and so the other ministers survived.

26 February 1936

An American writer, Hugh Byas, has called this period of Japanese history, 'Government by assassination'. It reached a climax in the second month of 1936. The First Division of the Japanese army was stationed in Tokyo and had a large number of Imperial Way sympathizers in it. The junior officers were known to be getting restless, and they were in close contact with Kita Ikki, whose dreams of grandeur for making Japan 'ruler of the world' were getting wide publicity. Few of these officers had any connection with the old *bushido—*

samurai tradition of the Japanese army. Many had peasant backgrounds, and with only an elementary education, they were easy victims of ultra-nationalist propaganda. Senior army officers and members of the government were afraid of the way things were developing. So the First Division was ordered to Manchuria.

Before the order could take effect the junior officers acted. In the early hours of 26 February, during a blizzard, copies of a manifesto were delivered to all Tokyo newspapers. 'We believe', it said, 'that it is our duty to remove the villains who surround the Imperial Throne.'

Whilst this manifesto was being dispatched, 1,500 soldiers and officers below the rank of captain split themselves into bands of thirty and set out for the homes of the leading advisers to the Emperor Hirohito. Two former premiers were killed, Admiral Suzuki (who later became Prime Minister at the end of the Second World War) was stabbed and left for dead, and another of the Emperor's chief ministers was only just missed. The Prime Minister himself, the elderly Admiral Okada, was lucky. Awakened by loud noises, he had left his bedroom and hidden in a lavatory in the servants' quarters of the house; meanwhile the assassins had found Okada's brother-in-law and because he looked something like Okada killed him by mistake. The Prime Minister was reported dead and a guard mounted over his body which had been laid out quickly. Amid all the horror a touch of the bizarre occurred. Okada disguised himself in servants' clothes, put on large tortoise-shell spectacles and came out of hiding; he mingled with the small gathering of mourners and paid last respects to 'his' body!

Other key points were also seized. But two things went wrong. Some senior officers, on whom the juniors were depending, failed to give their support; and Emperor Hirohito, on whose behalf the revolt was planned, was enraged by the murders. When this was known, the generals moved. Troops were brought in from outside Tokyo, the Emperor's views publicized, and so within three days the mutiny was over. One hundred officers were court-martialled and fifteen shot, not with traditional and honourable rights, but quietly in batches of five. Kita Ikki was also executed. All this was at Hirohito's express command—but it was the last important decision he was free to make until 1945.

The fanatics had played their hand and failed. With the Imperial Way Group discredited, the Control Group of the army and its expansion-into-China policy emerged strong and dominant. The army now put massive pressure on the Japanese Cabinet, and to establish military power even more firmly, preparations for a war with China were hurried on.

The Dark Valley

Patriotic feelings were whipped up. Writers looking back over these events agree with the view that in the mid 'thirties 'Japanese nationalism became hysterical.' In 1935 the Japanese Foreign Office declared 'Japan' and 'Far East' would no longer be used: 'Nippon' and 'East Asia' were to replace the more usual European words. Money spent on teaching English in schools was cut, and in 1937 a forceful piece of official propaganda was published called *Kokutai No Hongi.* This short book put in dogmatic form what a Japanese should believe, and how he should act. Although a difficult book to understand it sold nearly two million copies in six years, and was imposed as a textbook in all senior schools.

The First Army Division leaves Tokyo for service in Manchuria after the February 1936 affair

Not all Japanese accepted the way things were developing. One diplomat in China asked to be recalled because of 'the arrogance of our military, who force their so-called Chinese "brothers" to kow-tow to them in the streets'. Another called the Japanese quarter of Shanghai 'a rotting sewage canal' which lowered Japan's reputation abroad even further.

At home Japanese liberals who believed in representative government called the 1930s the 'Dark Valley', because it was a period in which the army gradually took over control of affairs. For them Japan had, since 1915 and the Twenty-One Demands, taken a wrong turning; for them the spirit of *bushido* as Nogi, Togo and Yamagata understood it had become distorted. How distorted can be seen in the next chapter, when the impact of the ideas of *Kokutai No Hongi* on a Japanese officer is shown.

13 'I am a Patriot'—A Japanese Officer Speaks on the Eve of War

My Creed

I am a Patriot.
I believe in Yamato—my country.

It has been rightly said that,
'The valour of a Yamato heart
When faced with a crisis
Its mettle proves.'

A crisis threatens our national existence. My country has for centuries stood high above other nations and now that Nippon is about to make great strides, light and shadow seem to have appeared—we must stir ourselves to find a way

School day in the 1930s began with bowing to the Emperor's portrait, hidden from view in the white building

forward in these difficult times.
I believe in my Emperor.

> 'O that I could die
>> Beneath the Emperor's banner,
>> Though deserveless of a name.'

I am loyal and obedient to the Emperor: he is the symbol
of unity and I shall follow him implicitly. By implicit
obedience I mean offering my life for the sake of the
Emperor; this is not self-sacrifice, but a means of living
under his august grace. The Emperor is divine. In the legend
of the creation of Nippon the Sun Goddess decreed, 'As
endless as Heaven and Earth shall the Imperial Throne
prosper'. The Emperor Meiji wrote in his poem of 1910:

> 'Should we not preserve in dignity
>> This Land of Peace
>> Handed down from the Age of the Gods?'

Our history shows that through ceaseless efforts successive
Emperors have overcome every obstacle, expanded Imperial
enterprises and built up a good and beautiful nation.
I believe in my Family.

> 'Precious are my parents that gave me birth
>> So that I might serve His Majesty.'

My family is more important than myself—or any other
individual. Individualism is a way of thinking that makes
me, as a person, all-important. It is an evil Western idea.

My Fears and Hopes

My creed then is 'My Country, my Emperor, my Family'.
This creed is in danger. Its enemies are abroad and at home.

Across the Sea of Japan I fear Soviet Russia, now recovering
her enormous strength, and I fear that China may try to take
Manchuria from us. We must not sacrifice Manchukuo, won
by Yamato in a costly and bloody struggle. Far to the south
Britain and the United States have much wealth invested in
oil, rubber and other raw materials. As a result Nippon is a
'have-not' country. Nippon must challenge the old order by

expanding overseas. We must secure an equal distribution of the resources of the world.

At home there have been disastrous happenings in the last twenty years. Party politicians have brought dishonour to Yamato. Their behaviour has been scandalous. They take bribes from the big business houses like the rich Mitsui and Mitsubishi. I am convinced these city financiers have fixed both taxes and prices against the interest of the farmer. Industry and big cities mushroom, and they threaten the traditional Nippon way of life. They have brought to our country that other evil of the Western World—the Class War. My honourable father is a landowner and many of the men in my regiment come from sturdy peasant stock. We must preserve the values of the countryside against the destructive influences of the West: big business, trade unions, strikes, political corruption, luxury, dance halls and low moral standards.

Why we must act now

I stand for *Kodo-ha*, the Imperial Way. The nation is one vast family united in common loyalty to the Emperor. I shall be ruthless in supporting this. I am in deep sympathy with my fellow junior officers and with organizations like the Black Dragon Society and the Blood Brotherhood League. The Terror of the past few years was right; people must be made to see what is right. I am disappointed that our great effort of 26 February last year was not successful, but at least the army has some control and a strong voice in the government.

I believe things are changing for the better. I am told that it is only ten years since the prestige of the military in Nippon reached its lowest point. After the failure of the Siberian Expedition anyone in uniform was the object of pity or silent ridicule. The army had no tanks, aircraft or radio equipment. Older officers tell me they practised with paper models of aeroplanes stuck on bamboo poles, and rattled sticks to imitate machine guns. They had to carry out bayonet exercises barefooted to save their boots. Soldiers' food and fuel were scanty, and the barracks infested with vermin.

Now, only ten years later, the Army has achieved its rightful place in the making of national decisions. Senior officers will be important members of the government, and I think we have a Prime Minister, Prince Konoye, who sympathizes with our ambitions. Even if the politicians cannot agree, at least there is one man with the right idea. I hear that General Tojo has become Chief of Staff of the Kwantung Army. On his appointment on 1 March this year he sent a telegram to the General Staff in Tokyo which advised an immediate attack into China towards Nanking. I support General Tojo in this, for it is well-known that Chiang Kai-Shek's Nationalist Government of China in Nanking has just signed a pact with their enemies, the Chinese Communists. This pact can only mean one thing: the Chinese intend moving against our forces in Manchukuo.

It is in the national interest that we protect ourselves before it is too late. I am a Patriot.

14 Into China and a New Order in East Asia

The Marco Polo Bridge

There were two main Japanese armies on the Asiatic mainland in 1937: the Kwantung Army, which we have seen controlled Manchuria, and the smaller, 7,000-strong garrison army in Fengtai. This was an area just south of the Great Wall, near Peking, and the Chinese after some persuasion had accepted Japanese occupation of it in 1936. In the region was a network of railways which the Japanese army wanted to develop.

A land survey by the Japanese for commercial and military development had been made, but the local Chinese land-owners refused to sell some key plots. So the Japanese put pressure in the form of frequent and noisy army manœuvres on them. Trouble was obviously brewing, but there were no plans of attack by either side, such as the Japanese had had for Mukden in 1931. Most of this trouble came from the junior officers and the men rather than senior officers. In fact in the first week of July 1937 the Japanese Commander-in-Chief was seriously ill, and the general commanding the local Chinese soldiers was on leave.

On 7 July, during some night manœuvres by the Japanese near the Marco Polo Railway Bridge, to the south of Peking, skirmishing broke out. Tension mounted and the fighting became serious. Neither side was willing to give in. Three days later after an appeal from Fengtai, the Tokyo General Staff accepted that things had got out of hand, and agreed to send strong support from Kwantung and Korea.

Gradually this local clash widened into a full-scale invasion of China. The Tokyo government was headed by an easy-going man, Prince Konoye. He was very much a figurehead and had not the prestige and authority to order a withdrawal of Japanese forces. There was no real chance of a negotiated

81

Manchuria and North China 1931–37

settlement because the Chinese, having patched up the Nationalist/Communist quarrel, were determined to resist at all costs.

In August 1937 fighting spread to Shanghai and a three-month struggle for the city took place. China and Japan were at war in all but name.

The New Order in East Asia

By the autumn of '37 Japan had 150,000 troops in North China, and at the end of the year a military advance was made up the Yangtze River to Chiang Kai-shek's capital, Nanking. The curious thing about all this was that Japan was not ready for an all-out war. The expansion of her armed forces, begun in 1936, had hardly had any effect, and the Army General Staff in Tokyo and Prince Konoye kept hoping that the 'Chinese Incident' as it was called would soon end. But Chiang refused to give in, and with such a resolute Chief of Staff as Tojo the Japanese armies on the mainland became

A British view of Japan's invasion of China in 1937

DAWN OVER ASIA

intoxicated with the prospect of a great and decisive victory over the Chinese.

Nanking was captured, plundered and looted. The murder of civilians and the vicious treatment of women and children gained the Japanese soldiers a reputation for savagery. *Bushido*, with its code of chivalry, largely ceased to exist. For this and for the indiscipline of their troops the Japanese Officer Corps must take the blame. In 1938 Hankow fell, and then the Japanese extended their control into southern China by capturing Canton.

In November 1938 Prince Konoye broadcast to the Japanese people. Chiang's government, he said, had been 'reduced to a local regime'. Now Japanese aims, he went on, will be 'not the conquest of China, but co-operation with her'. This was Japan's 'New Order in East Asia'. The Chinese, however, were not taken in by this; it looked very much like the Twenty-One Demands in disguise. They decided to fight on.

Chiang's refusal to accept defeat posed serious problems for Konoye's government. Japan still had the cream of her army in Manchuria and could have continued with an offensive deep into the centre of China, but at home the Japanese people were

The plight of civilians under Japanese air-raids. A Shanghai street shelter in 1937

becoming weary of the 'China Incident'. Clothing and shoes were getting very short and taxes were rising. It seemed to the man-in-the-street that Japan was fighting an endless colonial war. Protests from the western powers, France, Britain and the United States about Japanese interference with their peaceful trading in China did not help either.

Then came the outbreak of war in Europe in September 1939. By the end of the following year Japanese militarists were cheering as 'their friends the Huns swept forward into France'. But some awkward questions had to be answered. If the Germans won a total victory in Europe, how would they view Japan's 'New Order in East Asia'? What about the British, Dutch and French colonial areas in South-east Asia: would Hitler take them into his Third Reich Empire?

Japan decided that she must lose no time in staking her claim to them. French Indo-China and British Malaya, with their rice, rubber, coal and tin resources, and the Dutch East Indies with its rich oil supplies, were the object of Japanese ambitions. The 'New Order' in Manchukuo and China could then be extended to form one immense 'Greater East Asia Co-Prosperity Sphere'—a common market area in which Japan would be the controlling nation. In 1941 no European power could do much to stop Japan. Only the United States had a fleet big enough to challenge Japanese seizure of these rich areas.

' *The Razor* '

In July 1941 Japan moved troops into French Indo-China and the threat to the rest of South-east Asia was clear. The United States immediately put an embargo on Japanese goods entering her country, and trade came to a standstill. If Japan moved further, would the United States fight? If they did, had Japan the military resources for such a war?

Prince Konoye decided these were impossible questions to answer and resigned. He was succeeded as Prime Minister by a man whose military record and character did not give much hope for peace: General Tojo. When faced with a problem Tojo was a believer in the sharp use of force rather than negotiation as a solution. For this he had earned the nick-name, 'The Razor'.

What went wrong in the 1930s?

On the eve of Pearl Harbour and the final breakdown of American–Japanese relations, it is worth taking stock of Japan's position.

What Japan's government wanted was the recognition by the United States and the West European colonial powers (Britain, Holland and France) of Japanese 'hegemony', or leadership, in East Asia. The United States in particular was unwilling to do this. We have seen how in the 1930s Japan slowly came under the control of the militarists, who had no real idea of what was best for Japan. Tojo and his government have been called 'short-sighted mediocrities' because they had managed to get themselves into such a corner that they must either accept humiliation and 'lose face' by withdrawing from China and Indo-China, or gamble on war.

In the eyes of these militarists there were three arguments in favour of going to war. Yet each was really only half-true.

First, Japan was overpopulated. Its chain of mountainous islands had only 16 per cent of land for cultivation and so its rising eighty million people needed room to expand. However, although Manchukuo was given much publicity as a 'breathing space' for the surplus population, hardly any emigration in

General Tojo in 1941

fact took place. A magnificent scheme to colonize the area with a million Japanese families never went beyond the paper stage; only a few hundred shopkeepers and railway officials moved in.

Secondly, it was argued, Japan did not have enough raw materials to develop her industry, and one of the prizes of war would be the rich monopoly of trade in south-east Asia. This was the most serious miscalculation of all. Since 1900 Japanese prosperity had grown by the 'multilateral' system (this is a term used by economists to describe a world trade fairly free from high tariffs). Under this system Japan could pay for her trading deficit in South-east Asia and Europe—where her raw materials and machinery came from—with the credit gained in the United States and China, where she sold large quantities of silk and cheap consumer goods. It was a most useful advantage for the Japanese to buy in the cheap south-east Asian markets and sell in places like the United States where they could get the best prices.

War with China, the United States and the British Commonwealth would destroy this advantage.

There was no one in Japan with enough influence to convince Tojo's government of the economic stupidity of war, especially when Britain and the U.S.A. were putting up tariff barriers against cheap Japanese goods. Looking back on things from today it could be argued that Japan should have changed her industrial production from shoddy, mass-produced articles to better quality manufactures and specialized equipment. But the militarists put forward *their* argument for war—the third one—saying that Japan needed something like the Greater East Asia Co-Prosperity Sphere, where her markets would be under her direct control. In the circumstances this sounded a reasonable case.

What really happened then? Although it was not to prove in Japan's economic interests to go to war, the Japanese aggressive spirit had been fostered by military fanatics for their own ends. Over the past ten years these men had been slowly edging themselves into a controlling position in the Japanese government. Now, in 1941, they sought to maintain their own political power whilst gaining glory for Japan by the conquest of an empire.

One writer says, 'Patriotism had been corrupted into immoderate ambition.' Perhaps when you have read the next few chapters you may come to the conclusion that the Japanese leaders were blinded by their own propaganda.

15 Pearl Harbour and Singapore

The Breakdown of Negotiations

'Japan is like a fish in a pond from which the water is gradually being drained away', a senior naval officer told Emperor Hirohito in 1941. The American trade embargo of 26 July was the crisis point in American–Japanese relations. They had been getting worse for some years because the United States, as a protest against Japanese aggression in China, had been slowly applying a most effective stranglehold on Japanese trade. First planes, then chemicals, then scrap-iron and aviation-spirit had been denied to the Japanese. Now, with their move into Indo-China, American, British and Dutch shipments of oil to Japan ceased. Oil was the vital product of the embargo. Japan imported 88 per cent of her needs—80 per cent coming direct from the United States.

Only one faint hope remained: negotiate with the United States. But Admiral Nomura, the Japanese ambassador, had been doing just this for over twelve months. Nomura was a man of principle and was known to oppose war, but he was out of touch with Tokyo where anti-American feeling was hardening. He received one message which clearly showed that the Japanese did not trust the U.S. It said, 'the U.S. is like a cunning dragon, seemingly asleep'. There was no way out of the deadlock. President Roosevelt said America would only raise the embargo if Japan opened peace talks with China. Yet when Tojo became premier there was no yielding on China. Cordell Hull, the American Secretary of State, called Japan 'a bandit nation'. He said later, 'We had reached the point of clutching at straws.'

Day of Infamy

On Sunday, 7 December 1941, Commander Itaya led the first formation of Japanese planes across the Hawaiian island of Oahu. He recorded, 'Pearl Harbour is still asleep in the morning mist.' A few seconds before 7.55 a.m. one of his planes flew low over Ford Island in the middle of the harbour, and a bomb exploded on a seaplane mooring. 'In those few seconds', one writer says, 'the United States and Japan passed from a precarious neutrality to 1,364 days of war.'

Within three minutes the navy H.Q. had broadcast a message to the United States mainland: 'Air attack on Pearl Harbour. This is no drill.' There were ninety-four ships in the harbour and the Japanese knew which ones they particularly wanted—the eight giant battleships on the quays off the south-east shore of Ford Island.

An eye-witness wrote:

'Over this great fleet the forty Japanese torpedo-bombers broke like a storm just before eight o'clock. They came in from every direction, each pilot carefully briefed on the particular angle from which to launch his torpedo in order to get the best run and cause maximum confusion in the defence. Taking the gunners by complete surprise, they were almost impossible to hit; in a few moments the harbour was criss-crossed by the white wakes of their missiles, and tremendous explosions were leaping up against the steel sides of the battleships.'

By 8.30 a.m. the *Oklahoma* had capsized, the *West Virginia* had been sunk, the *California* was beginning to sink and the *Arizona* had blown up, killing four-fifths of its crew of 1,500. The other four battleships were severely damaged. When the cost was counted the Americans found that 90 per cent of their air and sea power in the mid-Pacific had been immobilized or destroyed.

Pearl Harbour has become one of the best known events of modern times, and there are already many legends about it. Two of them, however, one American and one Japanese, will not stand up to close examination.

First, the Americans claimed Japan struck deliberately

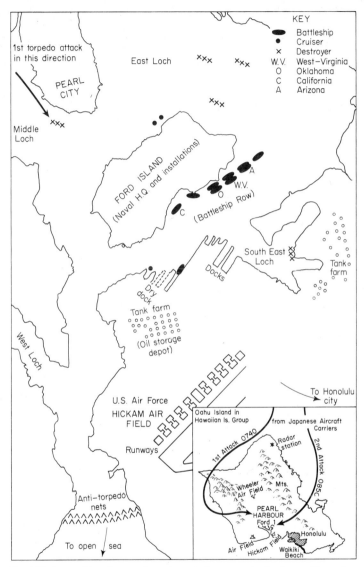

Pearl Harbour with an inset to show the main Japanese air attacks on 7 December 1941

without warning. In a speech to Congress Roosevelt called 7 December 'a day that will live in infamy'. Yet there is some evidence to show that this was a cover for United States incompetence. As early as January 1941 J. C. Grew, America's ambassador to Japan, warned Washington that the Japanese were 'planning to go all out in a surprise mass attack at Pearl Harbour'. U.S. Naval Intelligence received the message and recorded, 'We place no credence [faith] in these rumours.' After the war forty fat volumes gave details of an investigation into 'Why the U.S. was caught napping'. The conclusion was that she had simply not made adequate preparations against a possible attack after the negotiations broke down in the summer of '41. Tragically for the Americans it was also revealed that two American privates manning a radar station on the north shore of Oahu had twice reported planes to the north around seven o'clock on 7 December. Their officer did nothing because he thought they were American planes on an exercise. Fifty minutes warning was lost.

Japan for her part claimed a total victory. 'This day world history has begun anew', wrote one Japanese. But this was a dangerous exaggeration, and like the American claim, was a cover for shortcomings. The attack on Pearl Harbour was meant to destroy United States power to interfere in a Japanese push southwards from Indo-China; however Japanese military intelligence had grossly over-estimated

The *Arizona* a short while after the ammunition magazine exploded

American naval strength. It was later admitted by the U.S. Navy that it would not have been strong enough to attack a Japanese defence ring in south-east Asia. A more serious charge against the Japanese was that they attacked the wrong targets! Certainly they destroyed a battle force, but they missed two things which were to cost Japan dearly later on. They failed to search for several American aircraft carriers which were not far out of harbour on manœuvres, and the Japanese planes neglected Pearl Harbour's oil storage tanks and the repair shops. So Pearl Harbour was not a total victory, and was probably unnecessary. What it did do was to bring an angry and determined America into the war.

Singapore

The island fortress of Singapore was the citadel of British power in the Far East. For years it had been hailed as invincible. The day after Pearl Harbour, whilst other Japanese forces were attacking Hong Kong, the Dutch East Indies and the American-held Philippines, General Yamashita began an advance southwards down the Malayan Peninsula. His aim: to capture Singapore within three months. Yamashita had been a member of the Imperial Way Group in the 1930s, and after its disgrace in February 1936 had found promotion difficult. But he was an outstanding commander, so Tojo reluctantly agreed to his taking charge of the Malayan campaign. In seventy-three days Yamashita achieved Japan's greatest military triumph. His troops, well-trained and equipped for jungle-fighting, infiltrated and outflanked the ill-prepared British forces. A British officer explained how the Japanese managed their rapid movement:

'It's like this. Before the war our colonel using a map would say, "Now this is thick jungle here, and this is mangrove swamp; we can rule this out. All we have to concern ourselves with is the road." Thus we kept to the roads everywhere. Why, I went through a mangrove swamp the other day, and nowhere did I go down in the mud over my ankles. Anyhow you can walk on the roots in almost any swamp.'

And this was exactly what the Japanese infantry did!
One line of Singapore's defences disappeared when Malaya

The Malayan jungle where the British and Japanese fought in 1942

fell to Japan so quickly. Its second line of defence was naval power. But this crumpled when the British battleships *Repulse* and *Prince of Wales* were sunk—they had tried to take on a Japanese fleet without fighter escort. Singapore surrendered in February 1942.

Within six months Japanese forces had used their air and sea superiority to seize huge areas rich in raw materials. All they had to do now was to hold them. But the Japanese found that, in common with many other wars of conquest, it was one thing to take an area, and quite another to keep it . . .

16   Midway Atoll: The Tide Turns

A Battle is Planned

In 1942 Midway Atoll was the outer defence point of Hawaii and Pearl Harbour, which was now the only important naval fortress left to the Americans in the central Pacific. The atoll has two small islands, the larger only two miles long. The Americans had built an airfield there, and the whole atoll was honeycombed with defences. Pearl Harbour lay 1,100 miles to the south-east, and Japan, in the other direction, was about 2,100 miles away. On 4 June 1942 a spectacular and decisive battle was fought on the high seas for control of this lonely atoll. It was also a curious battle in that the ships of one side never saw the ships of the other. The catastrophe at Midway marked the turning of the tide in the Pacific War, and was as important as El Alamein and Stalingrad in the war against Hitler.

By the spring of '42 the Japanese had established themselves along a perimeter which ran from Burma round the East Indies to New Guinea, then turned north through the Pacific islands to the east coast of Siberia. Within it they had inexhaustible supplies of food and raw materials. These, the Japanese thought, put them in a position to fight on indefinitely—so the Americans and British were bound to ask for a compromise peace.

Japan's immediate ambitions concerned New Guinea and northern Australia, and, to gain freedom of action here, they needed to remove what was left of the American naval threat in the Pacific. So the seizure of Midway was planned in the hope of compelling the remaining American warships to give battle. However, unknown to the Japanese, some of their operational secrets had leaked out, and their Combined Fleet

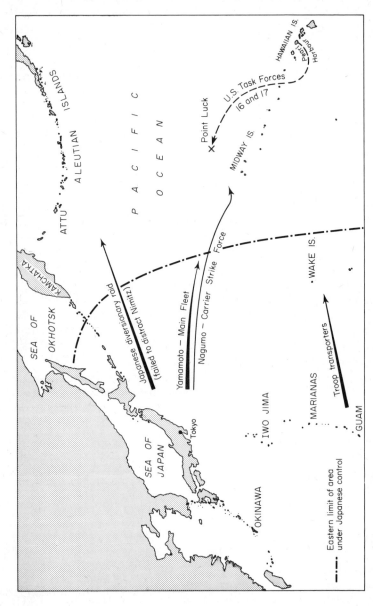

Preparations for Midway

was going to be drawn into an American trap. This trap had only the slimmest chance of success. Its author was Admiral Chester Nimitz.

Nimitz was in a desperate situation. An error of judgment or plain bad luck and the American war effort in the Pacific was finished. His personal reputation was also at stake, for he had been promoted to the top command after the Pearl Harbour disaster over the heads of twenty-eight more-senior

Admiral Nimitz, planner of the United States Midway operation

officers! His biggest need was ships. He had only three aircraft carriers, no battleships and eight cruisers plus a number of smaller vessels.

Nimitz planned his campaign from Hawaii. Because U.S. Naval Intelligence had broken the Japanese radio code, he knew that an island called 'AF' was to be attacked. Was 'AF' Midway, or Hawaii or perhaps somewhere else? To find the answer he used a trick: a fake message in ordinary language was sent from Midway to Pearl Harbour saying the atoll's freshwater plant had broken down. Two days later a

Japanese radio message in code was intercepted, which when translated said 'AF' was low on water.

Nimitz was aware that he was putting all his meagre resources into the Midway operation—but he had to surprise the Japanese who would not expect him to do anything until Midway had actually been attacked. So at the end of May 1942 he divided his ships into two Task Forces and sent them to Point Luck, a map-position about 350 miles north-east of Midway. The plan was to launch carrier aircraft against the Japanese left flank before the American ships were themselves sighted.

Opposing Nimitz was one of the most formidable naval forces assembled in modern times: ten battleships, eight aircraft carriers, twenty-four cruisers and a fleet of over a hundred supporting vessels. One of the Japanese battleships was the *Yamato*, a 63,000 ton colossus with guns which could fire a broadside of thirteen tons of steel shell! The Commander-in-Chief of the Japanese Combined Fleet was Admiral Yamamoto. His determination had developed Japan's carrier-based air strength, and it was these aircraft carriers that Nimitz most feared. Four of them, the *Akagi*, the *Kaga*, the *Soryu* and the *Hiryu*, made up the First Carrier Strike Force under Admiral Nagumo. These ships were to clear a way for an assault on Midway by an intensive air bombardment. Yamamoto's main fleet, some 200 miles to the rear of Nagumo, would then come

Admiral Nagumo

in, occupy Midway and prepare to meet the expected American naval attack. As we have seen, the Americans had already moved. The U.S. carriers, *Hornet* and *Enterprise* in one Task Force, the *Yorktown* in another were on their way to Point Luck.

The Japanese are Ambushed

Nagumo's ships were first spotted 200 miles south-west of the American carriers at dawn on 4 June. Nagumo had already launched an air attack against Midway. Into this he put over half his planes, keeping the remaining ninety-three armed with torpedoes just in case some enemy ships were in the vicinity. At 7 a.m. Nagumo was told that the attack on Midway was not heavy enough and another was necessary. He hesitated. Fifteen minutes later he made a fatal decision: he ordered the ninety-three planes to change their torpedoes for bombs. Then at 7.28 a reconnaissance plane reported that American ships had been sighted. Nagumo panicked were any of these ships 'carriers'? No one knew. He dare not risk sending a second air attack against Midway, so he reversed his order. The result was chaos. The first wave of planes had begun returning from its Midway bombing and wanted to land, refuel and rearm; but the second wave was still on deck in the middle of arming with bombs or changing back to torpedoes.

Nagumo was caught in a web of events over which he now had little control. The presence of American carriers was confirmed and came as a shock. He had not anticipated that enemy surface ships could appear so soon. In fact, the *Hornet's* aircraft were already on their way, to be followed soon by the dive-bomber squadrons of the *Yorktown* and *Enterprise*. The battle of Midway was about to be joined.

Phase One: The Tragedy of Squadron 8

Torpedo Squadron 8 took off from the *Hornet* just after eight o'clock in the direction of Nagumo's carriers, some 160 miles away. It was supported by some fighters which climbed high above the bank of cumulus cloud, whilst Lieutenant-Commander Jack Waldron, leader of the squadron, stayed low with his heavy-bellied planes, and cruised along at 110 mph. Strict radio silence was kept so as to surprise the enemy. When

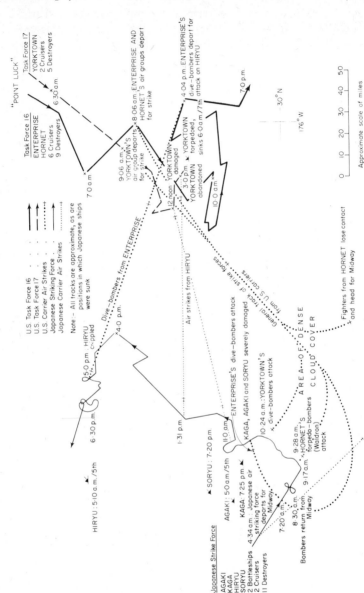

The Battle of Midway: timetable of events 4 June 1942

Waldron sighted the Japanese they were much farther to the right than he expected, and as he wheeled away into attack he lost his fighter cover above the clouds. To make a torpedo attack a plane must come in low, flying steadily through intense anti-aircraft fire with no flinching. As the approach is made pilots must rely heavily on their own fighters to keep the enemy's planes away, hoping also that the pom-pom gunners on board the ship are poor marksmen. But Waldron and his squadron were unlucky. The Japanese carrier commanders had each managed to put some Zero fighters into the air, and these got onto the tails of his squadron pilots long before torpedo-release point. Squadron 8 was massacred. Of fifteen planes and thirty crew only one man survived.

Jack Waldron, commander of Torpedo Squadron 8

Phase Two: A Destructive Morning

The Japanese triumph was short-lived. For the next hour urgent preparations for a full-scale counter-attack against the Americans continued. One after another, planes were re-fuelled, hoisted from the hangars and quickly arranged on flight decks. On Nagumo's flag-ship, the *Akagi*, all seventy of her planes had their engines warming up as the big 36,000-ton carrier turned into the wind for launching. Within five minutes all planes would be airborne. Mitsuo Fuchida, a Japanese officer, gives us an eye-witness account of what happens next:

'Five minutes! Who would have thought that the tide of battle would shift so completely in the brief interval. At 10.24 the air-officer flapped a white flag, and the first Zero fighter whizzed off the deck. At that instant a look-out screamed, "Hell-Divers!" I looked up to see three black planes plummeting towards our ship. The silhouettes of American Dauntless dive-bombers grew larger. I fell intuitively to the deck. The terrifying scream of the dive-bombers reached me first, followed by the crashing explosion of a direct hit. There was a blinding flash and then a second explosion, much louder than the first. I was shaken by a weird blast of warm air.'

The *Akagi* had taken two direct hits. Normally they would not have been fatal, but further explosions of fuel and munitions devastated whole parts of the carrier. As fire spread through the planes, lined wing to wing on deck, their torpedoes exploded. The entire hangar and deck area became a blazing inferno. The time was 10.46.

The *Kaga* and the *Soryu* were badly damaged from similar attacks; only the *Hiryu* escaped the onslaught. Efforts to save the three carriers were doomed to failure. On the *Akagi* even the chemical fire-extinguishers failed to work, and the blazing hell on the top decks meant that men deep in the ship's engine room could not get out. By twilight the *Kaga* resembled a gigantic torch lighting up the evening sky. All three carriers sank within the next twenty-four hours.

What had gone wrong for Nagumo? First, by the confusion which he himself had created early in the morning, the

Japanese had lost valuable time in preparing an attack. Secondly, the Zeros which had so successfully dealt with Waldron's squadron were taken by surprise, because they were not patrolling above the clouds and therefore missed the high-altitude dive-bombers of the *Enterprise* and *Yorktown*. Thirdly, as Fuchida said, 'We had been caught flat-footed in the most vulnerable condition possible, decks covered with planes armed and loaded for an attack.'

Phase Three: The Yorktown

The final phase of Midway took place during the afternoon. The fourth Japanese carrier, the *Hiryu*, had sheered off and in the hour before noon launched her planes for a counter-attack on the Americans. They found the *Yorktown*, and seven planes penetrated the carrier's fighter screen. A bomb put her boiler-room out of action and she became dead in the water. Repair parties got her going again but the Japanese sent in a second torpedo attack; two hit her port side and the *Yorktown* heeled over so far that there was serious danger of her turning turtle. She was abandoned.

Men struggle to keep their feet on the carrier *Yorktown* as it lists badly in the Midway battle

Meanwhile the Americans on the *Enterprise* prepared to attack the *Hiryu*, and what had happened to the *Yorktown* now happened to the Japanese carrier. She was bombed, disabled and scuttled.

Results

Midway was decisive. Tactically it was revolutionary, for it proved that carrier-borne aircraft were the vital weapon in the Pacific. Yamamoto had sent Nagumo and his four finest carriers as an advanced guard, and their loss cost him 75 per cent of his total air strength. Without adequate air cover he could not risk bringing the main fleet to Midway.

Strategically, Midway was far-reaching. We saw at the beginning of the chapter that plans for New Guinea and Australia depended on the defeat of the American navy in the Pacific. Now these were abandoned.

It is clear that Nagumo was over-confident. He was suffering from a 'victory' disease—he had been responsible for the Pearl Harbour attack, the sinking of the *Prince of Wales* and the *Repulse* off Singapore, as well as a score of merchant ships, all without loss of a major Japanese ship. But now lacking adequate knowledge of the enemy's strength, he had committed a military blunder. He had allowed four carriers, all close together, to be ambushed. After Midway, fatigue and gloom overtook the Japanese navy. An officer described Yamamoto's 'ashen face, in which only his strangely glittering eyes showed his feelings'. Defeat was bitter. The men could not even drink the beer and saké which had been loaded on board their ships for the expected victory celebrations. This was Japan's first defeat at sea since 1592.

17 Japan in Retreat

Social and Administrative Failure

In theory the Greater East Asia Co-Prosperity Sphere had been a dream which in 1942 seemed to be coming true: the ending of western monopoly of trade in the Far East. More generally it meant the collapse of white supremacy, which was poked fun at. A south-east Asian newspaper, the *Syonan Times* had a paragraph in its edition of 25 February 1942, 'Wherever the victorious Nippon armies have brought the New Order, Europeans may be seen, naked to the waist, doing jobs that Asians only were made to do before. Many of them cut ludicrous figures, slouching their way through work which even Asian women are able to do with greater ability.'

Far Eastern countries were now looking to Japan as the superior nation—the 'light of Asia, the guide and teacher of her peoples'. The Japanese found that many Burmese, Malayans, Thais and others were willing to co-operate and to believe Tokyo radio propaganda when it claimed to be freeing them from western exploitation.

Then, slowly, the real meaning of Japanese power in Southeast Asia became apparent. Local leaders had to do what they were told, and any opponents were tortured by the despised Kempeitai, the Japanese military police. A Burmese complained to his people: the British who were 'sucking blood out of you' had been replaced by the Japanese who 'are here to suck the marrow out of your bones'. In Malaya guerrilla bands formed against Japanese domination and savage reprisals were taken should villages give shelter to these bands.

In 1942 a railway was planned to join Burma and Thailand across 300 miles of jungle and mountainous country. It was constructed by manual labour only, because there was no proper engineering equipment. Food and medical supplies were practically non-existent. Prisoners-of-war of all races and coolie labourers from Burma were compelled to work through monsoon conditions. 63,000 died of disease and starvation.

So early sympathy and co-operation turned to hatred and

THE DELIVERER

"Have no fear: I come to set you free from your chains."

Japan poses as champion of Asia against the chains of the imperialists (1942)

underground resistance. All over East Asia the 'New Order' collapsed because the Japanese failed to keep the good will of the newly-conquered areas. It was their most serious blunder.

Japanese officials were seen to be not only less efficient than the British or the Dutch or the Americans, but also greedy and ignorant. Japanese soldiers too made bad use of their authority. There was little control from Tokyo or from many senior officers, and the army became a byword for brutality and stupidity. As at Nanking in 1938 the junior officers and combat troops were the worst. The Japanese Foreign Minister, Shigemitsu, admitted later how weak the home government was in these matters of discipline: 'I had no actual authority; I did my best, but these men paid little heed even to orders of their superior officers.'

Military Failure

Japan under-estimated the powers of recovery of the American and British Commonwealth armed forces. This, together with the social and administrative failure, destroyed any chance she ever had of gaining recognition for her 'New Order' in the Far East. At Midway she had seen the result of her failure to bomb the naval repair shops at Pearl Harbour. Then from the midsummer of '42 the Japanese fought, for the first time on a large scale, soldiers as determined and as well-trained as her own. The industrial power of her enemies meant also that within months she would be up against the most modern military equipment.

After Midway the Japanese High Command decided its ring of defences would not be complete until all New Guinea and the Solomon Islands were under control. But it was here that the Australians and the Americans took up a struggle which was to prove as decisive on land as Midway had been at sea. Japan wanted Port Moresby as a naval base and her troops reached a point within thirty miles of it before the Australians stopped them and began to push them back slowly through the New Guinea jungles and mountains. Through, says one observer, 'a stinking jumble of twisted, slime-covered roots and muddy 'soup', where disease in the form of black-water fever, scrub typhus, ringworm and yaws, was as dangerous as the human enemy. Here the Japanese suffered their first defeat on land in modern times.

Five hundred miles to the east an equally savage land and sea battle was going on between American and Japanese troops for the island of Guadalcanal in the Solomons. Here after six months of toil, suffering and terror for both sides the Japanese retreated. An American wrote of the Canal, 'We were fighting no civilized knightly war. We cheered when the Japanese were dying. We were back to the primitive days of Indian fighting on the American frontier, no holds barred, no quarter given.'

Scraps of conversation between soldiers give an impression

of the war in human terms:
'My God, *you* still alive!'
and
'Yeah, there wasn't enough left of Bill to bury at sea.'

Further north a new technique of warfare developed which proved disastrous to Japan's control of the mid-Pacific. It was called 'island-hopping'. Only key bases with harbours and airfields were selected and attacked by the Americans; other islands, although occupied, were by-passed to be dealt with later. As a result Japan lost the strategic points of Kwajelein, Saipan and Guam by August 1944. And by December of that year General Douglas MacArthur, Commander-in-Chief of the American forces in the South-west Pacific, was back in the Philippines. Here the Japanese made a last attempt to break American naval power. Around Leyte Gulf, south of Luzon Island, a long and close contest took place, but the Japanese eventually withdrew northwards.

These were serious military reverses for Japan. Their commanders' ideas had become too rigid—they failed, for instance, to deal with submarine attacks on their shipping and they only adopted the convoy system after great losses. The loss of the Philippines meant that direct communication between Tokyo and the East Indies was cut. Furthermore, the capture by the Americans of Saipan in July 1944 gave them an island only 1,300 miles from Tokyo—the city was now well within range of enemy heavy bombers.

Part of Tokyo after the devastating March 1945 fire-raid. More people died than at Hiroshima; a bigger area destroyed than during the 1923 earthquake

In Burma and India Japan paid the price of the over-
confidence and jubilation which had spread through her
forces after the capture of Singapore. British and Indian
troops rapidly learned the lesson of previous defeats, and with
jungle training and improved air power they met the Japanese
army on the Imphal Plain just inside the Indian frontier from
Burma. For two months a decisive and costly struggle went on
around the village of Kohima, but by the summer of 1944 the
Japanese were retreating back to Burma.

The Saipan and Imphal disasters forced Tojo to resign, and
for a brief moment in Japan there was talk of a compromise
peace, but the militarists were still very powerful in the government and the war went on.

Kamikaze

Now at the end of 1944, after two-and-a-half years of slow and
bloody fighting Japan had lost almost all the territory she had
won in those six triumphant months after Pearl Harbour.
Everywhere she was retreating.

In the thirteenth century a typhoon which wrecked a
Mongol invasion of Japan was called the 'Divine Wind' or
Kamikaze. In 1945 the Japanese formed suicide squadrons
which were given this name again. They were a last resort.
Kamikaze pilots, with their tunic buttons engraved with a
special, honoured insignia, the three-petalled cherry blossom,

A remarkable photograph of a *Kamikaze* attack on the American ship *Missouri*,
on 8 May 1945

were told: 'Your mission involves certain death.' They were to take their planes loaded with explosives and dive straight at the targets.

In the struggles for the islands of Iwojima and Okinawa, only hundreds of miles from the Japanese mainland, losses on both sides were catastrophic. All 23,000 Japanese on Iwojima, a tiny volcanic island only eight square miles, died. Nearly 100,000 were killed in the battles on Okinawa. The Americans had over 60,000 casualties, many of them on the 400 ships attacked by *Kamikaze* pilots off Okinawa.

In June 1945 the island fell to the Americans. The Japanese commander left a poem before committing suicide:

> 'Though with the last arrow gone,
> My blood dyes Heaven and Earth,
> My Spirit shall return, shall return
> To defend the Motherland.'

For the Motherland was on the verge of collapse.

What was it like for Japanese civilians? Incendiary bombs had almost destroyed central Tokyo and many other cities. Gwen Terasaki, the American wife of a Japanese diplomat, recorded one experience in her diary:

'Before the war there were no beggars in Japan. But today I saw a man grab into the dustbin, like an animal, spilling litter out. He found some food clinging to a paper wrapper, and he pressed the paper tightly against his face to gnaw the food away. Then a dog dived into the reeking pile of refuse, scavenging side by side with the man.'

But for one city worse was yet to come . . .

18 The Terrible Fame of Hiroshima

'Unconditional Surrender'

An extract from a Japanese diplomat's diary for New Year's Day 1945 reads: 'This is the year of decision. Sad though it is, we must face realities squarely. We have lost the war.' In 1945 the facts of defeat were clear to many people, and on 6 June of that year the first open clash between the 'peace party' and the 'war party' took place. Back in 1943 Roosevelt and Churchill had made their policy one of 'unconditional surrender'. But the Japanese had no idea what this might mean in practice. The peace party in the Japanese government led by Marquis Kido thought an effort should be made to meet British Commonwealth and American leaders to see if, at least, the Emperor would be allowed to keep his throne and position after the war. But the militarists argued that the fate of the nation was at stake. Anami, the War Minister, wanted a defeat of Americans on Japanese soil *before* terms were sought. Anami carried the day, and the war dragged on.

The Americans themselves were divided on the issue of how to end the war. Three groups made their voices heard to the President. First, there were those who wanted a combined assault on the Japanese mainland. General MacArthur was known to favour this, with a direct thrust at the industrial heart of the country around the Tokyo Plain. Secondly, there was a group of men who favoured negotiation. They thought that the demand for unconditional surrender would prolong the war. If only the Japanese—a proud nation—could be told that they would be treated favourably, surely the fanatics could be overthrown and peace made. A third group knew of the existence of a secret weapon, which they hoped could shock the Japanese into immediate surrender.

The Secret Weapon

Since the early 1940s, American scientists like Enrico Fermi and Robert Oppenheimer had been researching at Los Alamos, in New Mexico, on a bomb which used atomic energy. Estimates of its power in 1944 were the equivalent of only 500 tons of TNT; by May of the following year the figure was raised to 1,500. (The actual bomb had a power of 20,000 tons.) Despite this miscalculation the United States was well aware of the importance of such a weapon. The Secretary of War said, 'It might turn out to be a Frankenstein monster that would devour all, or a blessing that would make the world secure.'

Events were reaching a climax. On 16 July 1945, in the desert of New Mexico, a group of men was taken to within twenty miles of a bomb-test zone, and each was given a strip of very dark glass. One of them wrote later:

'This glass is so dark that at mid-day it makes the sun look like a little, under-developed, dull-green potato. At exactly the expected moment I saw through the dark glass a brilliant ball of fire, which was far brighter than the sun. I saw it expand slowly, and begin to rise, growing fainter as it rose. Later it developed into a huge mushroom-shaped cloud, and soon reached the height of 40,000 feet.'

The first atomic bomb test had taken place.

Ultimatum

Ten days later President Truman and Winston Churchill issued a declaration from Potsdam in Berlin, where the future of the defeated Germany was being settled. They called on Japan to surrender. Knowing about the secret test they threatened that 'the alternative for Japan is prompt and utter destruction'. The full text of the Potsdam Declaration was picked up by a Japanese radio-listening station at 6 a.m. (Tokyo time) on the 27 July. A quick examination by the Japanese Foreign Office revealed a ray of hope for the peace group. Clause 10 said, 'We do not intend that the Japanese shall be enslaved as a people or destroyed as a nation'; also, the vital term 'unconditional surrender' was mentioned only once, and that with reference to the armed forces. There was now growing support for peace talks to save at least the Imperial form of government, and Prime Minister Suzuki hoped that Soviet Russia, at present neutral, would act as mediator.

Despite all this the *New York Times* of 28 July gave the following banner headlines to Japan's reply,

JAPANESE OFFICIALLY TURN DOWN ALLIED SURRENDER ULTIMATUM

It was clear that the Japanese militarists were still strong enough to get their own way. They pinned their hopes on the one-and-a-half million men in the Japanese Home Army, and they said they had enough oil and ammunition left for just one great battle. In it *Nippon Seishin* (the mind, soul and spirit of Japan) would give them victory.

August 1945: little was left standing in the Japanese urban and industrial centres of Tokyo, Nagoya and Osaka. Eight million people were homeless, and their food ration was pitiful. Edible weeds, which were normally used as chicken food, often replaced rice. A black-market flourished. A four-pound bag of sugar should have cost a single yen; it actually cost 260 yen!

'. . . *nothing left to burn*'

The time on the watches of the aircrew of the U.S. B.29 Bomber, the *Enola Gay*, showed 2.45. It was early on 6 August, and the take-off was dangerous because the single atomic bomb-load was very heavy. It took skilful piloting by Colonel Paul Tibbets to get the necessary upward lift from the specially lengthened runways of the small Pacific island of Tinian, near Saipan. Only two observation planes accompanied the *Enola Gay*. The flight was uneventful, and the aircraft arrived in a cloudless, blue sky over Hiroshima at eight o'clock in the morning.

Hiroshima was an important industrial city in southern Japan, and had suffered very little bombing. Its quarter of a million people were beginning to go about their daily activities, and took scant notice of a few planes high in the sky. At

8.16 a.m., and at 31,600 feet the atomic bomb was released, and it exploded just before it would have hit the ground. A Japanese journalist wrote later:

'Suddenly a glaring, white-ish, pink-ish light appeared in the sky accompanied by an unnatural tremor which was followed almost immediately by a wave of suffocating heat and a wind which swept away everything in its path.

'Within a few seconds the thousands of people in the streets and the gardens in the centre of the town were scorched by a wave of searing heat. Many were killed instantly, others lay writhing on the ground in agony from the intolerable pain of their burns. Everything standing upright in the way of the blast—walls, houses, factories and other buildings—was annihilated and the debris spun round in a whirlwind and was

The centre of Hiroshima (about a thousand yards from the explosion) a few weeks after 6 August

carried up into the air. Trams were picked up and tossed aside as though they had neither weight nor solidity. Every living thing was petrified in an attitude of indescribable suffering.

'Beyond the zone of utter death in which nothing remained alive houses collapsed in a whirl of beams, bricks and girders. Up to about three miles from the centre of the explosion lightly-built houses were flattened as though they had been built of card-board. The few who succeeded in making their way to safety generally died twenty to thirty days later from the deadly gamma rays.

'About half an hour after the explosion, whilst the sky all around Hiroshima was cloudless, a fine rain began to fall on the town and went on for about five minutes. It was caused by the sudden rise of over-heated air to a great height, where it condensed and fell back as rain. Then a violent wind rose, and the fires extended with terrible rapidity, because most Japanese houses are built only of timber and straw.

'By the evening the fire began to die down and then it went out. There was nothing left to burn. Hiroshima had ceased to exist.'

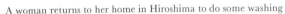

A woman returns to her home in Hiroshima to do some washing

Months later the Red Cross were still dealing with the lasting horror: those condemned to death by the gamma rays, which destroy the white corpuscles in the blood. One Red Cross doctor noticed the clock in the railway station at the edge of town—the fire had stopped the hands at just after a quarter past eight. He wrote in his diary: 'It is perhaps the first time in the recorded history of humanity that the birth of a new era has been recorded on the face of a clock.'

The Emperor Acts

This was a moment of unparalleled crisis for Japan. Reports were flooding into Tokyo, but they could give not much more than a smattering of the reality. Then at 1 a.m. on 9 August the Soviet Union, until now neutral, invaded Manchuria. The Red Army was hurrying to be in at the kill. When the news reached America a United States Senator said: 'Apparently the atomic bomb which hit Hiroshima also blew Joey [Stalin] off the fence.' Ten hours later on the same day a second

Hiroshima in the winter of 1945–6. A woman crosses the Aioi Bridge near the explosion point. The 'Atomic Dome' in the background was one of the few structures to survive in a half-mile radius

American atomic bomb turned half of Nagasaki into 'a city with not a tombstone standing'. Over other cities millions of leaflets were dropped by American planes to persuade the Japanese that their cause was hopeless.

Immediately the Emperor Hirohito called a Supreme War Council meeting in an air-raid shelter deep under the Imperial Palace. The Prime Minister, Suzuki, pressed the Emperor to accept the Potsdam Declaration if the Imperial authority could be preserved. Anami, the War Minister, tried to insist on more special conditions, such as 'no enemy occupation'. The Emperor himself broke the deadlock by saying that Potsdam must be accepted as his people had suffered enough. Messages were sent to Japan's enemies.

President Truman of the United States did not like having the Imperial Throne condition attached to the Japanese reply, but he was also very worried at the entry of Russia into the war. The Red Army was already 200 miles deep into Manchuria. It was plain to the Americans that Stalin wanted to extend his territorial influence in the Far East exactly as he had done in eastern Europe. This Truman wanted to avoid at all costs. Also he knew the American public wanted peace—even on Japan's terms! The *New York Times* of 11 August had bold headlines,

G.I.s IN PACIFIC GO WILD WITH JOY. 'LET 'EM KEEP EMPEROR' THEY SAY

The American reply, on behalf of all the allies, said that from the moment of surrender Japan would come under the control of SCAP—the Supreme Commander of the Allied Powers, General Douglas MacArthur.

15 August 1945

The Emperor read the reply and at a conference of his ministers gave his decision: surrender. Hirohito now recorded a statement to be broadcast to the Japanese people at noon the next day, 15 August. Would the militarists accept the Imperial authority? Some did not. Early on the 15th a final, desperate revolt was organized by a small group of army officers. They had the support of Admiral Onishi, the founder of the *Kamikaze* suicide squadrons. He had said a day or so before,

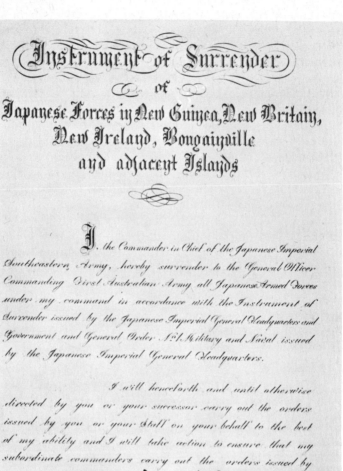

The surrender document of the South-East Command of the Japanese army

'Let us formulate a plan for certain victory. If we are prepared to sacrifice twenty million Japanese lives in a special attack by *Kamikaze*, victory shall be ours.' An attempt was made to seize the record of Hirohito's broadcast. But order was restored by soldiers from the main army Headquarters in Tokyo, which refused to have anything to do with the fanatics. Onishi and Anami committed suicide.

The Emperor's message went out over the radio. Whilst he admitted Japan had not been victorious, no mention was made of defeat. In a now famous understatement Hirohito declared, 'The war situation has developed not necessarily to Japan's advantage.' The official surrender to MacArthur took place aboard the U.S.S. *Missouri* early in September, whilst

A Japanese delegate signs the official surrender document aboard the *Missouri* in Tokyo Bay, September 1945 (MacArthur is on the left in shirtsleeves)

throughout the Pacific Japanese military units were made to sign individual surrender agreements, thus ensuring they all accepted Hirohito's decision (see the document opposite).

Gwen Terasaki has an entry in her diary describing how the Japanese looked on the last day of the war:

'There was a stunned apathy on the faces of the people in

119

the street. Everyone was starving, few had the physical stamina even to express their thoughts coherently. The people were shabby, hungry and often physically unclean, without the fuel and soap for the bath that is the daily necessity and pleasure of every Japanese. There was a sadness in every face, and a kind of tired relief.'

19 Japan During the American Occupation

The Japanese begin to live with defeat

The United States Navy entered Sagami Bay and dropped anchor near Tokyo at the end of August 1945. General MacArthur called it 'the greatest gamble in history', because, although the Japanese had capitulated, serious trouble was expected from rebellious army units and civilian extremists. 8,000 seasoned American troops, who had been taught to think of the Japanese as cruel and treacherous, landed cautiously. They were surprised at the general peacefulness. In fact suspicion was mutual. Most Tokyo families stayed under cover for fear of persecution. Reporters recorded that the children were the first to break the barrier of hostility when sweets and bubble-gum were offered by American G.I.s.

The problem of reconstruction was enormous. Nearly five million homes were in ruins. Total destruction, for instance, in Nagoya, Japan's third largest city, was calculated at 89 per cent. Families crowded into dugouts, or slept in hallways, whilst employees often slept in their offices. An American observer described Japan briefly as, 'devastated, hopeless, flat-broke and leaderless'.

A British interpreter has given us a longer account of Tokyo in the last months of 1945. The middle part of the city, around the Imperial Palace and the old business area was battered but the concrete buildings were more or less intact. Outside this core 'everything has gone and all you see for miles around is nothing but a vast sea of ashes; no bits of walls, no cellars even, just ashes'. The outer suburbs had escaped, but tiny houses there, originally intended for two people, now had four or five families living in them. Prices were very high. A pair of shoes made of material not much better than thick brown paper cost 900 yen—about £15, or the equivalent of a family's total expenditure for one month before the war.

Food was so scarce that people began going by train out into the countryside to barter with the farmers. Hours were spent in ticket queues at Tokyo's Ueno Station by men and women with small parcels of household oddments which they hoped to exchange for rice. 150,000 would leave everyday and return the same evening, in carriages from which the seats had been removed to make more room—even the running boards and buffers were occupied.

A queue at Ueno Station, Tokyo, in 1946; the people are leaving the city to barter goods for rice with the peasants

SCAP

One of the things the Japanese had accepted when surrendering was a 'military occupation'. In theory it was a joint allied duty, but in practice it became an American task, with the real power of making decisions given to one man: this was MacArthur, the Supreme Commander for the Allied Powers (SCAP). He carried a high military reputation with him to Tokyo, where he set up his headquarters in a building beside the Imperial Palace moat. His admirers pointed to his commonsense and efficiency in dealing with immediate problems like demilitarizing Japan, repatriating three million Japanese soldiers from abroad, organizing speedy imports of foodstuffs and putting on trial some Japanese accused of war crimes. But MacArthur had his critics. He was vain and aloof. He lived, they said, 'above the clouds', because he never attempted to check how his decisions were put into practice. He rarely left Tokyo and never toured the countryside. He also resented any interference with his 'rule', and this made for poor relations with his Government in Washington.

The real efficiency of the American occupation rested with the large administration which MacArthur brought with him —the 30,000 'Occupationnaires', as they were called. The Japanese had no illusions about MacArthur's rule. The *Nippon Times* wrote: 'If we must have a military government, why not our own?' But the Americans were determined to prevent this at all costs, by keeping to the terms of the Potsdam Declaration to 'strengthen the democratic tendencies among the Japanese people'.

Hirohito and Yoshida

The Americans' first thought concerned the status of Hirohito. Personally he was a shy man, keenly interested in marine biology, but during the war he had become to Japan's enemies 'a sinister international menace'. In 1945 one of his cousins advised him to abdicate, saying 'he was the captain of the ship [Japan], and he must take the responsibility for its going aground'. But his heir, the Crown Prince Akihito was only twelve years old and many Japanese were afraid he would become a puppet of the United States.

At SCAP headquarters some said 'Kick out the Emperor'; others wanted to humiliate this man they thought the Japanese worshipped—'de-god him', cried the G.I.s. MacArthur, however, avoided the problem. He would not, he wrote, 'outrage the feelings of the Japanese people, and make a martyr of the Emperor in their eyes'. Perhaps MacArthur saw himself as a kind of twentieth century Tokugawa Shogun, ruling the country himself with the Emperor as a figurehead.

So the Japanese kept their Emperor, but few Americans

could have foreseen his new image. It began with the photograph taken on 27 September 1945, which you can see below. Hirohito and MacArthur are standing side by side, and the contrast between the small, stiff Emperor in very formal civilian dress and the much taller American general in his casual open-necked shirt is obvious. A few Japanese thought MacArthur's appearance and manner were an insult to the dignity of their Emperor and that the photograph was a deliberate attempt to damage his prestige. Yet a feeling of sympathy arose in place of the old reverence for a semi-divine figure.

This feeling was reinforced when, as one Japanese put it, Hirohito 'came down from the clouds' and toured the country talking to the peasants in the fields and the workers in the

The photograph that caused the trouble: MacArthur and Hirohito meet on 27 September 1945

factories. An American magazine, *Time*, reported this tour and described Hirohito as a 'tense, shuffling figure in a grey overcoat and a crumpled hat'. This made him even more popular with his people—they seemed to be relieved that the Emperor was one of them.

Since 1950 Hirohito has been very much in the background of Japanese affairs. He is referred to as 'the Honorable across the Moat' (of the Imperial Palace), and only on rare occasions does he come into the public eye. Yet he commands considerable admiration from the Japanese people as a whole. On his birthday thousands jam the bridges leading to the Imperial Palace—they want to show their respect by signing the visitors' book!

Hirohito remains a shy, rather sad figure. In the grandstand of the Tokyo Olympic Games in 1964 he remarked to the U.S. ambassador how much he was enjoying himself: 'I fear', he said, 'I have been cut off too much from my people.'

American occupation officials in 1945 soon found that they could not work without the co-operation of the influential Japanese civil service and key members of the Japanese Cabinet. In the effort to bring democracy to Japan this was MacArthur's greatest problem. The Japanese parliament or Diet had always followed the lead given in debates by the Prime Minister, which meant that real power lay in the Cabinet. Japan's Prime Minister, Yoshida, made it clear that he wanted this tradition continued. He was acceptable to the Americans in 1946 because during the war he had been an 'anti-Tojo' man and he had a reputation for honesty. He soon became disliked by MacArthur as a 'bull-headed, testy autocrat', but this view was not shared by everyone. Japanese recovery after the war owed much to Yoshida, who stood up to SCAP dictation and had many of the more extreme schemes of 'Americanization' modified. As far as the Diet was concerned neither Yoshida nor SCAP could bring it to have a sense of responsibility. There were many scenes of brawling between members. In March 1947 one debate began a series of fights which lasted on and off for eleven days: the *Nippon Times* displayed a headline, 'Diet or Zoo', and called the whole affair 'a national disgrace'.

Three Issues: Land, Population Explosion, Education

In 1946 the Owner-Farmer Establishment Law was passed. SCAP insisted that large-scale ownership of land must cease. This not only fitted in with American ideas of equality, but broke up the powerful landowning group which had provided the fanatical officer corps of the 1930s with many recruits. By this law no man might own more than approximately seven acres. If he had more he must sell it at a low price to the government, who in turn sold it to peasant-tenants on easy terms. By 1950, 4¾ million acres had been purchased by over 4 million tenants. This was the most important and far-reaching law passed during the occupation. It completely altered the hopes and opportunities of millions of Japanese, who could now work on their own land; it brought, says one writer, 'a considerable increase in the sum of human happiness' in a Japanese village.

Japan has had a population problem for a long time: her 34 million of 1872 had risen by the mid 1960s to 98 million. Eleven million of this increase were born in the five years after 1945. To keep such a large number of people prosperous was difficult. After the war industry was expanded to provide more

Women queueing at a rice store in a village outside Tokyo, 1946

jobs and food production was intensified by careful, scientific farming. (In the 1950s for every one-and-a-half tons of rice which India produced per hectare—two-and-a-half acres—Japan could produce four tons). But all this effort only scratched the surface of the problem, because somehow the birth-rate had to be cut down. So in 1948 the Eugenics Law was passed, which made abortion legal. This meant that a Japanese woman by paying a small fee could, if she wished, have a pregnancy ended without serious danger to her health. Within a short space of time it began to have effect, and fifteen years later Japan's population increase was halved. In the next two chapters we shall see the importance of this for Japanese prosperity.

A Japanese family has always attached a great deal of importance to educational success, and this accounts for the high rate of literacy in twentieth century Japan. But for several years after 1945 she faced a critical shortage of buildings and textbooks. Many of the latter had been banned by the Americans because they contained military propaganda. The 'kind' of education was another problem. Bowing to the Emperor's portrait, for instance, disappeared in the forceful 'Americanization' of Japanese education, 'Subjects' were

Women's dressmaking school in Tokyo. Notice the American influence in the architecture

revised, and Social Studies replaced History and geography; civics, with its emphasis on a citizen's rights and duties, replaced the traditional Japanese ethics and its concern for manners and behaviour.

The Americans also insisted on a rapid expansion of university education, and Japan's seventy prewar colleges were increased to two hundred! But the only way for an ambitious Japanese student to achieve success and get a well-paid, important job was still to go to one of the old-established places. Tokyo University regularly had forty applicants for each place available.

Independence

Several things led to Japan's successful recovery during the six years after defeat. The commonsense of leading public figures like the Emperor, Yoshida and MacArthur; the hard work and initiative of many of the middle-ranking officials of the occupation; the willingness to co-operate of many Japanese, who seemed relieved that the American soldier was not the 'beast and devil' as described in Tojo's propaganda.

But to these three can be added a fourth reason—the one which gave speed to Japanese recovery. Between 1948 and 1951 a large amount of 'aid'—money, food, equipment and trade orders—poured from the United States into Japan, because America found she had need of a prosperous, co-operative ally in the North Pacific. These years saw the rise to power of Mao Tse-tung and the new Communist China. And American relations with Russia grew steadily worse. So with Japan as an ally the United States could feel more secure. The importance of this was illustrated in 1950 when the Korean War broke out between the North Korean/Chinese Communist forces and the United Nations. Japan became a strategic base for American troops who formed the bulk of the United Nations army.

In 1952 Japan became an independent nation once more, by the Treaty of San Francisco. But many Japanese resented the fact that the United States were still allowed to keep some of their troops there. They felt that the presence of *any* foreign soldiers cast doubts on Japan's ability to rule herself democratically.

20　Interlude: City Life in Japan in 1951

Impressions of a Suburb

In the mid-twentieth century 10 million people lived in Tokyo and its suburbs. Their environment was briefly described by a British visitor as 'a tortured use of space'. In 1951 a detailed survey was made by R. P. Dore of one Tokyo suburb of some three hundred households. He wanted to find out how the Japanese earned their living, ran their homes, amused themselves and above all how they thought about and treated each other, for by the 1950s nearly two-thirds of all Japanese lived in towns.

After the war the centres of these cities had been completely changed by new buildings and roads, but the suburbs, especially if they escaped the fire-raids of 1945, gave the impression of being over-crowded. In the Tokyo suburb surveyed in 1951 a few houses were neat and trim, with tiled roofs, porches, sliding doors of opaque glass and wide windows of white paper by day and wooden shutters at night. But many of the others were without gardens, and there was plenty of evidence of dilapidation: rotting boards hanging loose, paper partitions browned by the sun and jaggedly holed by children's fingers. In the narrow streets could be seen a mass of overhead electrical wiring, bedding pushed out onto upper window sills, and washing hanging on rows of bamboo poles. The roads were so badly surfaced that choking dust in the dry spring and frequent puddles in a wet summer irritated travellers. But the Japanese argued that their suburb was a place to live in not to look at!

Living Conditions

Japanese housing needs have always been very simple. Little furniture is used so a family is not necessarily overcrowded though the average house is much smaller than, say, western

129

people would find acceptable. Add to this the high value which the Japanese place on personal cleanliness, with the widespread habit of bathing regularly, and the filth and squalor so common to cramped city housing in the western world becomes the exception not the rule in Japanese cities. However, sharing a house was a regular feature of this suburb in 1951, but a family complained less about the general lack of privacy than the very restricted cooking, washing and toilet facilities. Many of these 'shared' houses had only one gas-ring in a tiny kitchen, and those who lived in apartments found a lavatory had to be shared between ten families.

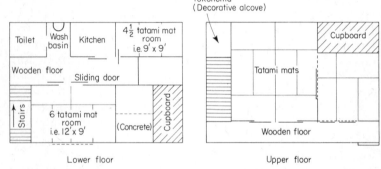

A typical home of a family living in a modern Japanese city

The plan above shows what kind of living space a family of five occupied (compare this with the farmhouse on page 56). One room was very like another and used for living and sleeping in. Heating was meagre because charcoal was expensive. In a ground floor room a table was placed over a boarded pit about thirty inches deep with a central hollow containing a charcoal burner; a thin quilt spread over the table frame prevented the heat from escaping, so that a person with his legs dangling under the table warmed the lower half of his body. In many houses this was the only form of heating.

Food

In 1951 the diet of the town-dweller differed only slightly from that of a traditional rural family. The years of occupation had seen some new ideas on nutrition spread by the schools and newspapers, but the Japanese still had only one word meaning both 'food' and 'rice'—*gohan*. Plain, boiled rice was eaten in large quantities and it gave 75 per cent of the calories needed to keep a man fit. The Japanese were very fussy about the type of rice; the small-grained Japanese variety was always preferred. But the milling process which produced the shiny white appearance also removed three-quarters of the vital vitamin B_1 content. The only other common foods were soup, to which soya-beans and dried fish were added to give good protein value, and vegetables, such as the giant white radish, pickled in salt.

However, the new ideas were beginning to have some effect. Bread was being eaten at breakfast as Japanese housewives found that release from the tedious rice preparation gave them a half-an-hour extra in bed! Some meat was eaten, but the traditional Japanese dislike of milk, butter and cheese remained. Butter in particular was avoided because of its 'repulsive' smell, which was thought to give people the body-odour of foreigners (the Japanese word, *bata-kusai*, means both 'foreigner' and 'smelling-of-butter').

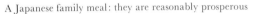

A Japanese family meal: they are reasonably prosperous

Although the real changes were yet to come, enough advances in diet and medical knowledge had been made to provide a startling alteration in expectation of life. In 1921 men and women could only hope for forty-two and forty-three years of life respectively; thirty years later the figures were sixty-one and sixty-five.

Patterns of Life and Change

Perhaps the biggest effect that city life has had on Japanese traditions has been in the family system. We saw something of this in Chapter 10. By 1951 it was clear that the old idea of the family working together had given way in the towns to simple wage employment in which the father went out to work away from the home. Thus the wife's authority there increased, especially as many of the new urban families had left their parents behind in rural areas. Even if the mother-in-law lived with a family, new 'authorities' challenged her power. The large weekly sales of women's magazines, for instance, spread modern ideas on hygiene and kitchen arrangements.

Also marriages for love became more common than those by family arrangement. This has been the biggest single change in Japanese family life in the twentieth century.

Although city life was slowly changing people's attitudes to life in general, R. P. Dore's investigations revealed that much of traditional Japan remained. Many of the old crafts were still practised: home workshops producing toys, umbrellas, writing brushes and clogs, flourished in the Tokyo suburbs and used family labour. Even the shops were family affairs and opened from 7 a.m. to 10 p.m.—chain stores being practically unknown.

Mass entertainment—baseball and spectacle films—was just beginning to affect the way people spent their leisure. However, in 1951 there were many instances showing the force of old social traditions and habits. Odd 'chats' with the neighbours during the course of a day's work, and evening visits to friends for a game of Japanese chess, cards or mah-jong were common. For the men there was an occasional visit to a geisha house for entertainment in the form of food, drink, dancing and feminine company which was trained to be amusing and attractive.

Family Portraits

So far only the overall pattern of life and change in this Tokyo suburb has been described. The last part of this chapter shows you something of the living standards of a few actual families.

Mr Oyama in 1951 was thirty-nine years old, and came from a poor family. The war had destroyed his house, and he now lived with his wife and three children in a one-room apartment. It was a 'four-and-a-half mat' room (that is, nine feet square) and had one cupboard; the *tatami* mats were yellow

Craftsmen re-covering *tatami*

and frayed with a musty smell showing they should have been changed long ago. The family property amounted to a table, two chests, some cooking pots, a wireless and one gas-ring. 'Cooking' for this family meant mainly preparing rice—they could only rarely afford meat—but fish and vegetables were added several times a week. One cold tap sink and one lavatory were shared with three other families. Under these conditions bathing was impossible (so the public baths were used), laundry difficult and the sanitation dangerous—the lavatory had no flushing mechanism, but it was connected with a sewer

133

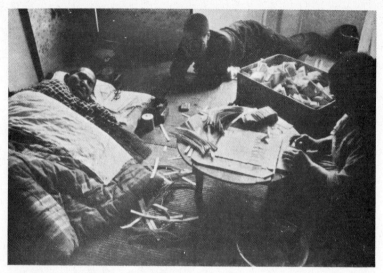

A poor family. The husband is sick and the household is supported by the wife's earnings from making match boxes at home

and was so arranged that waste water from the sink flushed the lavatory out every now and then. The dark and cold winter evenings kept the children indoors, and the difficulty of five people living in a tiny area of nine square yards was keenly felt. Here the noise and nagging created considerable family tension. The hope of Mr Oyama, who was an ordinary policeman on a low wage, was a house of his own.

Mr Kishi was a bank clerk. He and his wife (it was his second marriage) were satisfied with their standard of living. They had a two-storey, three-roomed house, with two gas-rings, a wireless, a bath, and a much-prized electric iron. In 1950 the house had been thoroughly repaired, with a leaking roof mended and some warped door frames replaced. Mrs Kishi was content in that the house was not overcrowded, for the children could sleep in a separate room from their parents. The family was able to spend money on such extras as cigarettes, newspapers, cinema and some home entertaining. Their food needs were modest, and they ate 'ration' rice (which contained barley and Siamese rice) rather than pay more for the pure white Japanese variety on the black-market, as some of their wealthy neighbours did. Most important to

Mrs Kishi was the fact that the rent, insurance and gas collectors had never been asked to 'come back next week' for their money.

Mr Takata was a wealthy company man, disliked by his neighbours for being brash, forceful and unscrupulous. His wife was a forbidding figure—she was a director of several companies of her own, entertained lavishly her business friends and was Vice-President of The Women's Economic Union. On the day of the first postwar election, when for the first time women were allowed to vote, she marched through the suburb at the head of a small army of servants to record her own vote, and to supervise the recording of theirs. The Takata household employed three man-servants, six maids, two secretaries, a carpenter and three chauffeurs; the house itself had twenty-nine rooms, one with a dance floor and grand piano. The material possessions of the Takata family represented the height of desire of the Japanese newly-rich: eighteen electric fans, two cars (American postwar models), a tiled bath that looked like a swimming pool, and, the real status symbol, a private telephone line to the local fire-station.

These then were some of the kinds of people to be found in any Japanese city in the mid-twentieth century. If you would like to know exactly how individual families spent their money in August 1951 you will find some detailed budgets on page 146.

21 The New Prosperity

The Changing Image

In April 1952 the Occupation ended. But only three days after the San Francisco Treaty had been signed dissatisfaction with the terms of independence led to serious and bloody rioting in central Tokyo. Threatening crowds gathered before the Imperial Palace and several attacks were made on foreign property in the city.

Yet in spite of this unpromising beginning, Japan settled down sufficiently well for her prosperity and progress to be so marked that terms like 'economic miracle' were being used to describe what happened by the mid 1960s. The Japanese are proud of their achievement, and see themselves as pioneers blazing a trail for the rest of Asia. Even more important for their pride is the removal of the international image of the 1930s—of the days when 'Made in Japan' meant that goods were shoddy and produced by low-paid workers in a sweat-shop.

More Money to Spend

We can best see the effect of a fifteen year rise in prosperity on the Japanese people by comparing a typical family budget of 1951 with that of the Sugimura family living in Tokyo in 1965.

The Sugimuras have two young children and a monthly income over the last year of about 49,000 yen (this would be nearly £50 as the rate of exchange is roughly 1,000 yen to the £ sterling). Mr Sugimura is the only wage-earner and he finds he can save nearly 20 per cent of his income, whereas in 1951 an average family could only just manage on their money if they planned things carefully. The rapid rise in wages in Japan over these fifteen years has given the Sugimuras a prosperous-looking standard of living. The amount they can save means that material things like cameras, transistor radios and electric washing machines, which would have been much sought-after luxuries before, are now regarded as natural possessions.

Evening shopping in a well-stocked grocery store in the 1960s

From the table overleaf it can be clearly seen that the Sugimuras dress well, and for this they rely on the bonus which many big industries pay to their workers twice a year—June and December. If a firm was doing well these bonuses could be as much as two months' wages. The father will have a business suit as well as several kimonos for evening wear; the mother will normally wear western-style clothing, for many city-dwellers argue that the Japanese kimono is 'expensive, time-wasting and uncomfortable'. A fair amount of the clothing expense is for personal grooming What is given to the barber and spent on cosmetics and hairdressing in a month could equal half the rent!

Rent for housing is often low because many industrial companies either provide the accommodation free themselves or subsidize their employees. Other 'fringe benefits' as they are called, besides the bonus and help with rent, are marriage allowances, hospital care and travel expenses to and from work. It is these which enable the Sugimuras to keep up a

standard of living higher than even the monthly budget sug-
gests. The growing number of department stores in the cities
display a wide range of goods for the Sugimura family to buy,
and profits show that business is brisk.

Monthly budget items for the family (in yen, 1,000 to the £)

1951		1965
7,000	Food	18,500
600	Housing, (Rent and Rates)	5,900
1,500	Clothing and Personal Items	5,700
700	Fuel and Lighting	2,300
500	Savings	12,000
3,700	Miscellaneous	4,600
14,000	TOTAL	49,000

Progress in Industry

Much depends on the employer for whom Mr Sugimura
works. The organization of Japanese industry shows that not
everyone enjoys the relative prosperity of this family. There
are three kinds of industry in Japan today. Scattered around
the big cities are small home-based workshops. They still provide a meagre living for hundreds of thousands of Japanese,
and consist of two or three benches and lathes in the family
living room. Also traditional centres of rural crafts have been
conveniently adapted for making small component parts—for
example, plugs and sockets for the gigantic Hitachi Electronic
Corporation—but such cottage industries are badly organized
and not very stable, as they depend on the city industries sub-
contracting (that is, letting out small orders for work).

Secondly there are the declining, but still large, industries
which made Japan a major manufacturing country in the
1930s: cotton textiles, sewing-machines, bicycles and cultured
pearls. Competition from synthetic textiles—nylon, rayon,
etc.—motor-cars and plastics has proved so strong that
employers, unable to modernize from declining profits, have
had to cut the bonuses paid to their employees.

The final group represents the great Japanese achievement
of the 1950s and '60s: iron and steel, lorries, ships, television

Kazaya Dam. Big projects like this provide much of Japan's hydro-electric power

and transistors, toys and cameras have gained a high reputation at home and in the world markets. In shipbuilding, for example, Japan outstripped Britain in 1956 as the world's leading construction nation, and by 1965 Japan was producing 44 per cent of the total world tonnage. This was the result of efficient management and recognition of what foreign buyers wanted. The Japanese have concentrated particularly on mammoth oil tankers, with many vessels over 150,000 tons, and even some of over 200,000 tons each, because these could be built efficiently by mass-production and assembly-line techniques. The camera industry, which began in 1945 by producing copies of the old-fashioned Leica and Contax cameras, quickly grasped the commercial possibilities of simple-to-use equipment. The firm of Nikon, for instance, gradually built up a good reputation and with others created a business boom in medium-priced, reliable instruments. In the 1960s a camera with 'Made in Japan' on its guarantee is backed up by an efficient, highly modernized industry. Japan's progress in electronics has been equally remarkable. This occurred because technical achievements opened the way to transistorizing all types of electronic equipment from radio and television sets to computers and telecommunication methods. Japanese production of transistor radios, which was

139

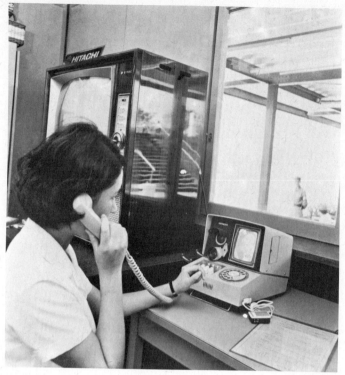

Japanese excellence in electronics: a Hitachi telephone-television

a mere six million in 1957, was increased to 250 million by 1963.

New Problems Replace the Old in the 1960s

Over-population has not been disastrous for Japan. The birth rate has gone down—the Sugimuras have only two children— because the Japanese have found that as society becomes more prosperous, married couples plan for fewer children. At the same time there has been a steady population movement from the rural areas to the cities in the last twenty years. By the mid 1960s a quarter of all Japanese people lived in the three great urban concentrations of Tokyo, Osaka and Nagoya. These people have provided the labour force for the rapid expansion of industry, and enabled stress to be put on exports which in turn paid for food imports. The Sugimuras still buy a

A startling impression of land terracing in Japan for rice cultivation

lot of rice, but they now eat five times as much meat and dairy produce as was usual in 1951. The drift to the towns has also eased the over-population of the countryside, but the peasant's standard of living remains a little lower than the city dweller's.

Japan's shortage of natural resources is slowly ceasing to be of prime importance with the development of synthetic substitutes like plastics. During the 1950s the Japanese Government tried to keep the coal industry in full production, but the coal was poor in quality, and found only in narrow seams. So Government aid was eventually reduced, although redundancies led to trouble at the pit-heads, and one strike went on for nearly two years with mounting violence. It has been found more profitable to increase coal imports and pay for them with exports of manufactured goods.

In 1961 the Japanese Government issued a Long-Range Economic Plan for the next decade. Ambitious targets such as trebling exports were mentioned, but Japanese business men were convinced that the expansion rate would slow down. The movement from rural districts to towns was becoming less rapid; as the industrial skills grew more complex long-term

The National Indoor Gymnasium, Tokyo. Notice the architecture

training schemes were needed; also Japanese organizations had learned as much about techniques as was possible from the advanced industrialized countries of Europe and America. In 1965 these fears were confirmed. Some industries began working below full capacity and with less profit. The economic boom seemed to have reached its peak, and the Sugimura family found that bonuses were not so large as before. A leading Japanese newspaper, the *Mainichi Daily News*, described the efforts of the Government 'to curb the over-heated economy'. In other words Japanese industrial expansion had been very rapid—perhaps too rapid for home and world markets to cope with.

Japan faced a crisis and many people became afraid. If a country produced many more goods than people wanted or could pay for, its industry had to cut down production. This resulted in unemployment. The lesson of the world economic crisis of 1929–31 seemed to say that the greater the boom the greater the crash.

The men in Japan's government and industry had two main solutions. First, the government deliberately expanded its programme of road and house construction and of improv-

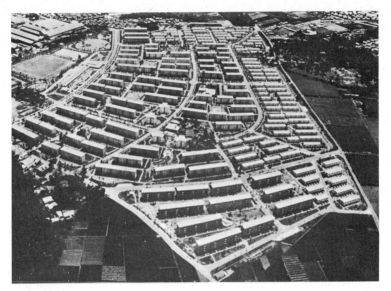

The big Hiborigaoka Housing scheme in the Tokyo of the 1960s

ing the telephone system. This provided alternative jobs for some workers who would otherwise have been out of work. Secondly, production of goods like TV sets was encouraged. In 1967 for instance Japanese television programmes went over to colour and a demand was created for new sets.

Both solutions proved successful, and by the summer of 1967 the threat of massive unemployment was over. Japan as a nation and the Sugimuras as a family could look to a more stable future.

'. . . when the big one comes'

In May 1967 a British journalist visited Japan and was very impressed by the general high level of prosperity there. But in a conversation with a retired member of Japan's government he asked about a serious problem: 'What happens when the big one comes?' It is a fact that a major earthquake can be expected in Japan roughly every seventy years. The last two were in 1855 and 1923, and so another can occur before the end of the century. The journalist recorded his conversation as follows:

143

'What would happen if anything like the 1923 earthquake recurred today, not only in Tokyo but almost anywhere in the densely populated belt of land along the Tokyo-Osaka line? "There have been some estimates," said my friend, "but they are so terrible that it is best not to think of them." I pressed him. The answer is that if an earthquake recurred in the same place as that of 1923, with the same force, at the same disastrous time of the day (just before noon)—and if fire caught hold of the city's oil storage tanks, while a million motor-cars blocked the streets, and perhaps a typhoon swept in from Tokyo Bay—well, then, over two million people might perish in the most terrible few hours of holocaust and horror and mass destruction since human history began, right there among the mighty industrial edifices (including atomic power plants) of a very major twentieth century civilization.'

22 The Japanese Character

Japan, like any other nation, is composed of individuals, who, though sharing the same nationality, do not necessarily act alike. There are certainly some obvious physical characteristics: Japanese men are slight in build, average 5 feet 5 inches in height, have straight black hair, dark eyes and what biologists call an 'epicanthic' fold on the eyelid, which gives the appearance of slanting eyes.

But is there a common character? Missionaries and visitors to Japan before and during the nineteenth century produced opinions as widely differing as 'charming, kindly, graceful' and 'suspicious, conceited, fickle'. By 1900 a typical western view was that the Japanese were 'mere imitators'. In 1946 Ruth Benedict, in her famous book *The Chrysanthemum and the Sword*, attempted to describe the Japanese. She said they had been well-trained from early childhood in a sense of duty: duty to the Emperor, to the nation, to the family and to one's good name. This is perhaps nearer to the answer. It seems that a Japanese prefers to be a member of a group, such as his family, rather than act individually. As such he has a high sense of personal honour and loyalty to this group, and it is still a serious matter in modern Japan to bring shame to the family.

Japan's rapid change to industrial and city life in the last half century has had great effects on the way her people behave. The older generation became critical of the behaviour of Japanese youth, and complained of the apparent decline in family loyalties. But there is a danger in accepting one generation's view of another and drawing permanent conclusions from it.

There have been many striking themes in Japanese history over the last century, some distasteful when measured in human terms, but others worthy of our respect and admiration. It is these themes which make up the total fabric of Japan's history as a modern nation.

Appendix

Three actual family budgets—August 1951

	A POLICE SERGEANT	A WRITING-BRUSH CARVER	A SMALL FACTORY OWNER
Number in the household	2 adults 3 children	2 adults 2 children	2 adults 2 children
	Monthly expenditure per person (excluding clothes) 1,000 yen to £		
	2,605	3,758	11,953
	Food (yen spent per person in family)		
Rice	509	331	792
Fish	96	167	544
Meat	47	81	869
Eggs, milk, butter etc.	6	31	330
Cakes	0	184	62
Vegetables	237	140	619
(Restaurant)	149	183	500
	Totals of all expenditure for whole family in one month		
Food	5,687	6,857	18,188
Rent, heat, light, water	997	261	1,708
Medical	2,413	220	920
Alcohol	0	480	6,400
Cigarettes	510	2,000	600
Entertainment	1,328	1,454	6,650
Religious gifts	50	250	100
Savings	300	4,031	2,100
Presents	560	325	2,300
Books	632	315	680
Clothes (paid with bonus)	1,935	16,210	5,150

Some Further Reading

Start with either of RICHARD STORRY's two paperbacks:
History of Modern Japan, Penguin, 1960.
Japan, Oxford U.P., 1965.
and E. SEIDENSTICKER, *Japan*, Sunday Times World Library,
1962—this is well illustrated. These three are easily obtainable
and are written in an interesting way for non-experts. If these
give you a taste for something more detailed try:
W. G. BEASLEY, *Modern History of Japan*. Weidenfeld and
Nicolson, 1963.

Japan's relations with China and America have dominated
some chapters of *Modern Japan*. Longmans' Modern Times
Series has two other books which link closely with this book.
D. B. O'CALLAGHAN, *Roosevelt and the United States*.
J. C. ROBOTTOM, *Modern China*.

From here a good way to get the flavour of modern Japan
is to look at some primary sources—travellers' tales, diaries
and descriptions of Japanese life:
JAMES KIRKUP, *These Horned Islands*. Collins, 1962.
GWEN TERASAKI, *Bridge to the Sun*. Joseph, 1958.
M. HACHIYA, *Hiroshima Diary*. Gollancz, 1955.
R. P. DORE, *City Life in Japan*. Routledge, 1958.
E. I. SUGIMOTO, *A Daughter of the Samurai*. Tuttle, 1966.

The one theme omitted from this book has been the cultural
scene. It is best to read or see aspects of this. As introductions:
DONALD KEENE, ed., *Modern Japanese Literature—1868 to the
Present Day*. Thames & Hudson, 1956.
GEOFFREY BOWNAS and ANTHONY THWAITE, *Penguin Book of
Japanese Verse*. Penguin, 1964.
and an impression of old Japan can be gained from seeing
some of the classic Japanese films of the 1950s.
Seven Samurai; The Gate of Hell; Ugetsu.

The Rank Film Library has recently put three very good
films in its catalogue:
The Miracle in Asia (No. 21.7643).
Harvesting the Land and Sea (No. 21.7644).
The Second World War, in 3 parts (Nos. 20.7649-50-51).
Write to Rank Audio Visual, Woodger Road, Shepherds
Bush, London W.12. for details.

The School of Oriental and African Studies, University of
London, London, W.C.1, issues a useful reading list.

Index

Index

Outline of Events

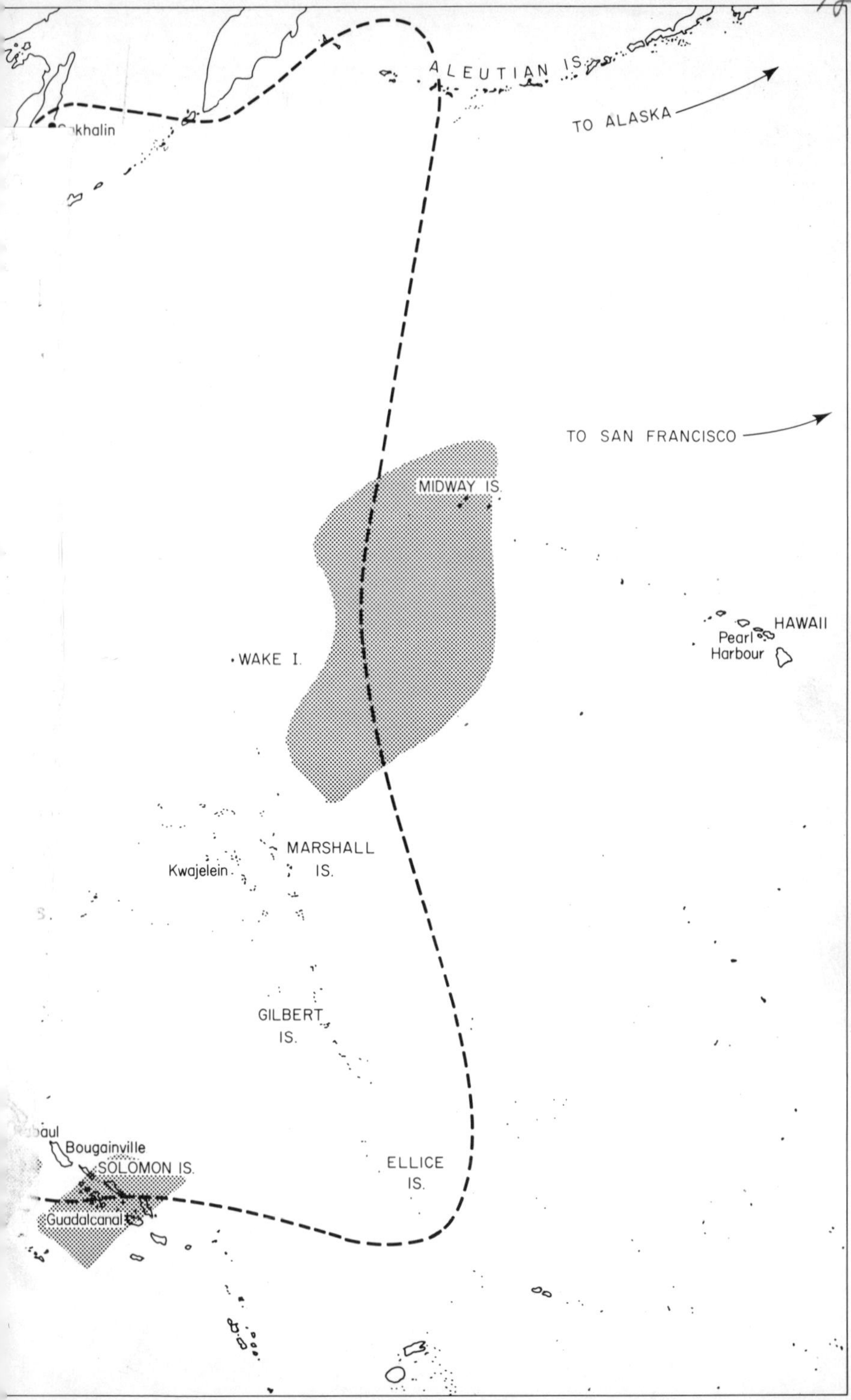
ALEUTIAN IS.
TO ALASKA
akhalin
TO SAN FRANCISCO
MIDWAY IS.
HAWAII
Pearl
Harbour
WAKE I.
MARSHALL
IS.
Kwajelein
GILBERT
IS.
baul
Bougainville
SOLOMON IS.
Guadalcanal
ELLICE
IS.